Woodcarving

The Beginner's Guide

Woodcarving

The Beginner's Guide

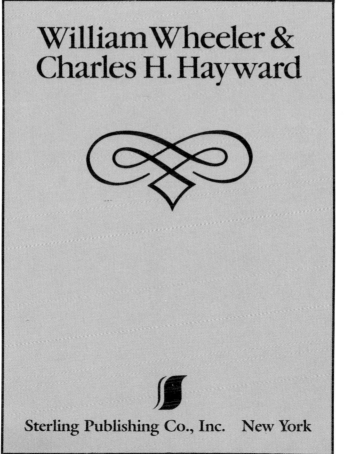

William Wheeler &
Charles H. Hayward

Sterling Publishing Co., Inc.   New York

10   9   8   7   6

Published by Sterling Publishing Company, Inc.
387 Park Avenue South, New York, N.Y. 10016
© 1972 by Evans Brothers Ltd.
Distributed in Canada by Sterling Publishing
% Canadian Manda Group, P.O. Box 920, Station U
Toronto, Ontario, Canada M8Z 5P9
Distributed in Great Britain and Europe by Cassell PLC
Villiers House, 41/47 Strand, London WC2N 5JE, England
Distributed in Australia by Capricorn Link Ltd.
P.O. Box 665, Lane Cove, NSW 2066
Manufactured in the United States of America

Sterling ISBN 0-8069-8790-1

Contents

Introduction

RECENT YEARS HAVE seen a marked growth of interest in wood carving, particularly amongst home craftsmen. Whether it be carving as applied to furniture, the production of small individual items, or the sculpture of large statues or similar items in the round, more people are practising the craft than at any time during the last three or four decades.

The fact is that there is no other subject which combines so ideally craftsmanship with artistic expression. Taking the former, wood is an exacting material which, although responding kindly to proper treatment, rebels furiously against bad handling. Its strong grain characteristics have to be understood and allowed for if the work is to avoid the limbo of failures and half-finished mediocrity.

On the artistic side, an appreciation of form, proportion, and balance is essential — in fact it is true to say that no excellence of technique can make up for lack of artistic expression. This, in truth, can be a danger, in that a student, concentrating purely on perfection of technique, may lose sight of the necessity for good design.

If these two basic requirements seem too exacting, the reader will find it a comfort to know that ability in both can be developed tremendously. Of the two, technique is the more easily acquired. It is largely a matter of practice. As in all work, skill to do comes of doing, and in fact in the last resort to get on with the job is the only way of learning. However, there are certain fundamental things which have been learnt over the years, and to know these may save the reader many hours of frustration and disappointment.

Artistic appreciation comes more slowly, and one cannot do better than examine good work, either of the past or the present, and endeavour to recognise the qualities that give it life and excellence. There are plenty of examples of carving to be seen in museums, churches, and other buildings, and if an endeavour is made to carve something in the same style or spirit it will not be long before an appreciation of quality is developed. It is the old story that true recognition of merit does not come until one endeavours to do something of the sort oneself. It is only then that one comes to realise the skill which the gifted artist-craftsman has put into his work.

The examples of work given in this book have been chosen with a definite end in view, to help both the beginner and the man who has had a certain limited amount of experience. In most cases the designs are drawn out on a grid so that the reader with little drawing skill can copy them map fashion, but it is emphasised that it is better for him to take them only as a basis on which to found his work, and to attempt to originate his own design as far as possible.

W. Wheeler
C. H. Hayward

Chapter one

Tools and equipment

s carved in chestnut.

There is an extremely wide range of patterns of carving tools—over a thousand—and it is puzzling for the beginner to make his selection. The fact is, however, that for average purposes only a relatively small number is needed. In the trade a carver may have anything up to eighty or so tools and of these he will have two to three dozen in constant, everyday use. The others he keeps for special purposes. When they *are* wanted, they are wanted badly, but they are seldom required in the general run of work.

The tools vary in three main ways:
Size: that is the width across the tool.
Length shape: whether straight or curved in length.
Section: the shape of the section: curved, flat, or V-shaped.

In addition there are other variations such as the spade, long spade, or whether the tool is shouldered or not.

The maid-of-all-work tool used by the carver is the straight gouge. It is fairly robustly made and will thus stand up to mallet blows. It is used in all bosting-in, setting-in, etc. At the same time it *can* be used for all types of carving, though the lighter and more delicate spade tool is more convenient for the final modelling and for special work.

Spade tools are tapered in length, and are of three types: the fishtail spade which has a quick taper; the long pod spade gouge or chisel of medium taper; and the long spade or allongee tool in which the taper extends along the whole length of the blade. All three types are illustrated on page 10.

The terms vary to an extent amongst different manufacturers, but those given are in general use. of three different angles (pages 12 and 13).

Straight tools. As shown on page 10, these are made in a wide range of sizes, and can be in the form of chisels, V or parting tools, or gouges. The last named are made in many degrees of curvature. The chisels may be ground straight across or they may be at an angle, in which case they are known as corner or skew chisels. Parting tools may be of three different angles (pages 12 and 13).

Curved gouges. These are needed mostly for fairly deep hollows, for instance when hollowing

9

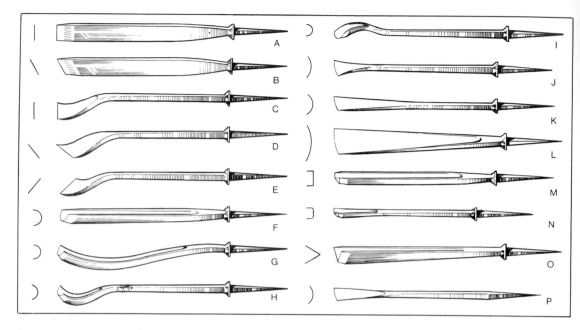

Fig. 1 Length shapes of chisels and gouges for woodcarving: **A** Straight chisel: **B** Corner or skew chisel: **C** Spoon bit or entering chisel: **D** Right corner spoon bit or entering chisel: **E** Left corner spoon bit or entering chisel (**C**, **D** and **E** are generally known as bent background tools or grounders): **F** Straight gouge: **G** Curved gouge: **H** Front bent or spoon bit gouge: **I** Back bent or spoon bit gouge: **J** Fish tail gouge or fish tail spade gouge: **K** Long pod spade gouge and chisels: **L** Long spade or allongee gouge and chisel (generally known as fish tail or spade tools): **M** Macaroni tool (also made curved): **N** Fluteroni tool (also made front bent): **O** Parting tool (also made curved, and front bent): **P** Unshouldered gouge and chisel.

Straight gouges and chisels are used for the general run of carving. They are the most robustly built type, and are invariably selected for bosting-in work and when the mallet is used.

Spade tools and long spade (or long pod as they are sometimes called) are lighter and are invaluable for modelling and final details. Fish tail gouges are the version in which really large tools are generally made. For certain hollowing-out operations (a bowl for example) the curved gouge is required. Similar in purpose, but for more acute hollow shapes, is the front bent gouge. An example of its use is in the hollow section of Gothic trefoils, etc. Back bent gouges are seldom needed, but come in for certain deeply recessed detail which could not otherwise be reached.

Carving tools are made in an astonishing range of sizes and patterns—there are in fact over a thousand of them. So wide a range has largely been brought about by personal preference (prejudice, if you prefer), though the particular requirements of certain trades may account for many patterns. The average professional trade carver usually has somewhere in the region of sixty to seventy tools, and of these perhaps twenty or so are in everyday, constant use, the rest being needed on special occasions. For the home craftsman a couple of dozen tools will meet nearly all requirements—he can in fact do great deal of simple work with far less. The bes plan is to select a basic kit of, say, a dozen too and add to them as occasion requires.

out a bowl. It will be realised that, although the straight gouge could be used in the preliminary stages whilst the shape is still shallow, it would begin to dig in below a certain depth because the handle could not be lowered enough to enable the bevel to be flat on the wood, Fig. 2A, causing grain tearing. By substituting the curved gouge as at Fig. 2B the bevel can lie flat.

Bent gouges. Of these there are two kinds: front bent and back bent (see page 10). The former is the more commonly used, and is required for cutting hollows in rounded shapes such as those found in Gothic trefoils, etc. Back bent gouges are seldom needed and should only be bought when the need arises (and this may never happen). Neither tool is required for the general run of carving.

Sectional shape of tools. These are known by numbers based on the Sheffield list. They are given on pages 12 and 13, and it will be seen that the same number is given to all straight tools of the same relative curvature regardless of width. As an example, a No. 9 tool is a straight gouge of semi-circular section no matter what its width. A No. 18 is a curved gouge, again of semi-circular shape and of any width. Thus when tools are ordered it is necessary to specify both the number and the width. To be on the safe side a full description can be given; for example: 'straight gouge No. 6, 8mm. ($\frac{5}{16}$in.)'; 'curved parting tool No. 40, 9mm. ($\frac{3}{8}$in.)'; or 'fish tail spade gouge No. 6, 13mm. ($\frac{1}{2}$in.)' It should also be stated whether the tool is to be handled or not. A slight complication is that some makers add a prefix to the number, but in such cases it is the last digit or the last two which count.

Handles. These vary considerably in shape. A few years ago the trade carver invariably used handles which were roughly hexagonal or octagonal in shape, Fig. 4A. They were cut by hand with a knife, and were invariably without ferrules. Various

---

Suggested kit for the man taking up carving:

Straight gouge No. 9, 6mm. ($\frac{1}{4}$in.); No. 9, 16mm. ($\frac{5}{8}$in.); No. 7, 6mm. ($\frac{1}{4}$in.); No. 4, 6mm. ($\frac{1}{4}$in.); No. 5, 13mm. ($\frac{1}{2}$in.); No. 3, 19mm. ($\frac{3}{4}$in.). Straight veiner No. 11, 5mm. ($\frac{3}{16}$in.); Straight corner chisel No. 2, 10mm. ($\frac{3}{8}$in.); Front bent chisel No. 21, 6mm. ($\frac{1}{4}$in.); Front bent R corner chisel No. 22, 3mm. ($\frac{1}{8}$in.); Front bent L corner chisel No. 23, 3mm. ($\frac{1}{8}$in.); Straight parting tool No. 39, 8mm. ($\frac{5}{16}$in.).

There is a certain amount of variation in the terms applied to carving tools, but those given here are in general use. In some cases the terms 'spade' and 'fish tail' seem to be interchangeable. Tools are usually obtained without handles, the latter being largely a matter of personal preference. Hexagonal or octagonal forms largely ut with a shaving knife by eye, and without rrules used to be popular in the trade, but have en almost entirely superseded by turned and ished handles.

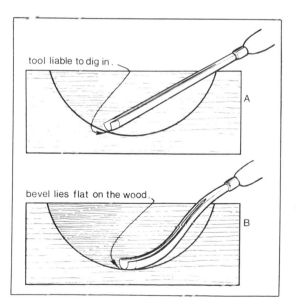

Fig. 2 Advantage of curved gouge on occasion. The straight gouge at **A** tends to dig in and chatter as the full depth is reached, whereas the curved gouge **B** follows the shape.

	STRAIGHT	CURVED	FRONT BENT	BACK BENT (up to ½in.)	1mm. ($\frac{1}{32}$in.)	2mm. ($\frac{1}{16}$in.)	3mm. ($\frac{1}{8}$in.)	4mm. ($\frac{5}{32}$in.)	5mm. ($\frac{3}{16}$in.)	6mm. ($\frac{1}{4}$in.)	8mm. ($\frac{5}{16}$in.)	9mm. ($\frac{3}{8}$in.)	11mm. ($\frac{7}{16}$in.)
CHISELS	1		21										
	2		22										
			23										
GOUGES	3	12	24	33									
	4	13	25	34									
	5	14	26	35									
	6	15	27	36									
	7	16	28	37									
	8	17	29	38									
	9	18	30										
FLUTERS	10	19	31										
VEINERS	11	20	32										
PARTING TOOLS	39	40	43										
	41	42	44										
	45	46											
MACARONI													
FLUTERONI													
BACKERONI													

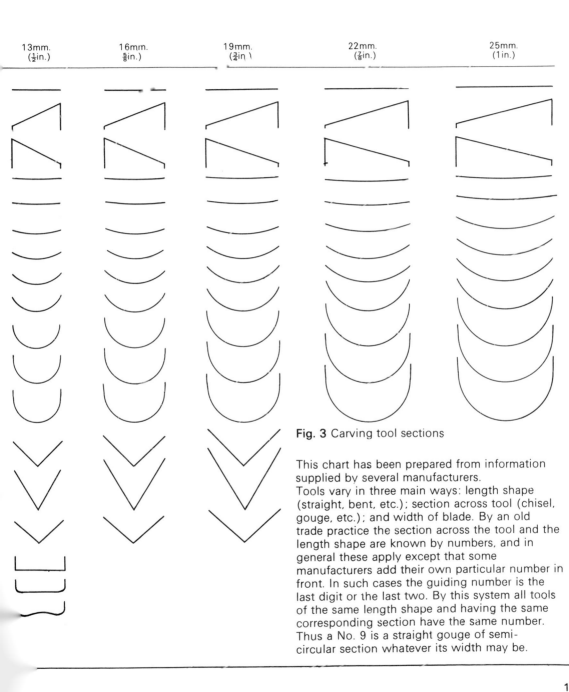

| 13mm. (½in.) | 16mm. (⅝in.) | 19mm. (¾in.) | 22mm. (⅞in.) | 25mm. (1in.) |

Fig. 3 Carving tool sections

This chart has been prepared from information supplied by several manufacturers.
Tools vary in three main ways: length shape (straight, bent, etc.); section across tool (chisel, gouge, etc.); and width of blade. By an old trade practice the section across the tool and the length shape are known by numbers, and in general these apply except that some manufacturers add their own particular number in front. In such cases the guiding number is the last digit or the last two. By this system all tools of the same length shape and having the same corresponding section have the same number. Thus a No. 9 is a straight gouge of semi-circular section whatever its width may be.

hardwoods were used; there is in fact a virtue in having a variety of woods or shapes so that a tool is quickly recognised. The carver may have thirty or forty tools laid out in front of him, and it is clearly a help to be able to spot the required tool quickly.

The 'South Kensington pattern', Fig. 4B, was usually in mahogany and originated in the school of carving of that name which flourished several years ago. The other handles, Fig. 4C and Fig. 4D, are the turned type now made almost exclusively. When all the tool handles are of the same pattern or wood it is a help to give each an easily identifiable mark, such as a touch of colour, so that they are easily picked out.

Mallets. These are invariably round in shape, as this enables the carver to strike from any direction without altering the grip on the handle. Sometimes beech is used, but, since it is the side grain that strikes the tool handle, it is liable to deteriorate quickly. A close-grained hardwood such as lignum vitae is much better and, being heavier, can be smaller. Weights vary from 1 lb. up to about $2\frac{1}{2}$ lb. Do not choose an unnecessarily heavy one as it can be most tiring in use. Large mallets are used mostly in big sculpture work where a great deal of waste may have to be removed with a large gouge.

Fig. 5 shows a pair of mallets and Fig. 6 a section showing how, in the best way, the handle passes right through the head and is wedged. Note also the curved shape where the handle passes into the head. This is much stronger than forming a square shoulder.

Rasps, files, etc. These are used chiefly in sculpture for the rounding of parts after the bulk of the waste has been removed with the gouge and mallet. The rasp is coarser than the file, and is used in the preliminary stages. The modern equivalent is the shaper (obtainable in two grades) which has the advantage of being non-clogging. The swarf passes right through. Rifflers are shaped files and may be needed to reach hollow parts. They are made in many sizes and shapes.

Punches. These are of two kinds; those to produce a textural effect on a background, and those of special shape for levelling the surface of awkward recessed parts. Examples of the latter are the small eyes cut in acanthus leafage which are of oval

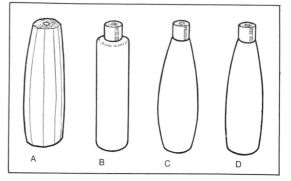

Fig. 4 Types of handles used for carving tools: A is the hexagonal or octagonal type: B the South Kensington pattern: C and D, the turned form.

Fig. 5 Woodcarver's mallets. The best are of lignum vitae.

14

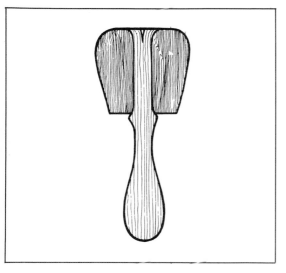

Fig. 6 Section. The shaft passes right through and is wedged. Note shape at top of neck.

Fig. 7 Abrasive tools used in preliminary shaping: **A** Flat shaper tool: **B** Round shaper: **C** Curved shaper: **D** Rasp: **E** File.

shape but pointed at one end (see Fig. 8A); or the sharply indented spaces between the berries of an astragal moulding Fig. 8B. A moulding of this kind is shown in Fig. 11, page 66. Sometimes a small recessed circle is required, and then the punch at Fig. 8C is used. The end of this may be flat or rounded according to the effect required.

It should be realised that the punch should be used only to sharpen up the surface after the recess has been cut with the gouge. It should never be used by itself, as the effect would bruise the wood and rob the work of its crispness.

Decorative punches are of many patterns, and may consist of dots, circles, crosses, etc., as in Fig. 9, and known as frosting punches. Of these the simple dot is the commonest. A punched ground-work is effective in some designs in that it gives the background an entirely different appearance or texture, and so emphasises the pattern, but it should never be used merely to hide up a badly levelled groundwork.

Routers. The hand router, or 'old woman's tooth', as it is sometimes called, Fig. 10, is used to ensure that a background is of equal depth throughout. Usually the groundwork is cut away nearly down to depth, and the router then used as a depth gauge to make the whole level. The flat chisels and grounders complete the job. The router can be specially useful when cutting raised letters to bring the groundwork to a constant level.

The portable machine router, Fig. 11, is an electric machine having a spindle and chuck which revolve at high speed. It can be fitted with a variety of cutters and can be used for flat recessing, piercing, moulding, rebating, or grooving. It saves a great deal of time in the preliminary removal of waste wood, or for working small mouldings. One

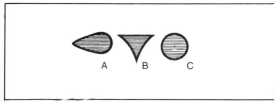

Fig. 8 Punch shapes.

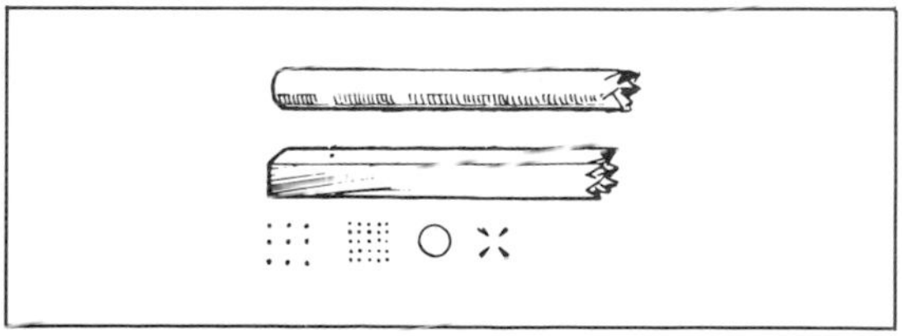

Fig. 9 Frosting punches.

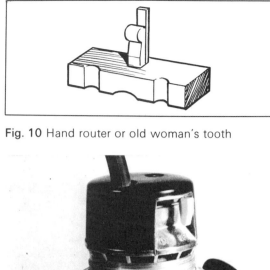

Fig. 10 Hand router or old woman's tooth

Fig. 11 Portable electric router. This can also be reversed beneath the bench top and used as a spindle moulder.

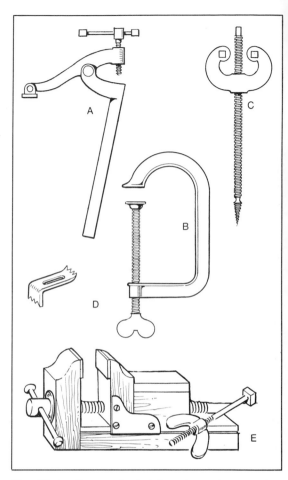

Fig. 12 Appliances for holding down the wood: **A** Bench holdfast: **B** G cramp: **C** Carver's bench screw: **D** Clips or dogs: **E** Carver chops.

special advantage is that it can be used equally well for shaped work. For instance, practically the entire section of the elliptical frame shown on page 91 was worked with the router.

Cramps, etc. These are used primarily to hold the work still whilst being carved. The holdfast, Fig. 12A, has a stem which passes through a hole in the bench, and the shoe (with a piece of waste wood interposed) is forced down on to the work. It is

specially useful when the fixing has to be done at a place which could not be reached with a G cramp at the edge.

G cramps, Fig. 12B, and thumb screws have their obvious uses, but are sometimes awkward in that they project from the surface and may be in the way of the tools or hands. In this case the carver's bench screw, Fig. 12C, is useful. The pointed end is screwed into the wood, being tightened by fitting

Fig. 13 Engineer's vice, invaluable for some work. The swivelling type is preferable as the whole can be turned without releasing the work.

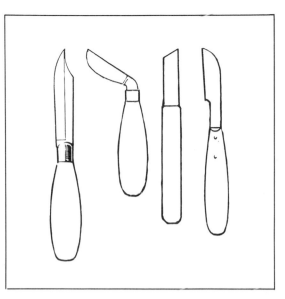

Fig. 14 Knives used in chip carving.

---

one of the square holes in the scrolled nut over the square end of the screw. The latter is passed through a hole in the bench, and the nut tightened beneath.

This device can be used when the wood is thick enough for the screw to be driven in without emerging at the front, and when a hole at the back or bottom does not matter. If the wood is too thin for this it is better to use the dogs, Fig. 12D, these being screwed to the bench.

Vice. The wood vice used by carvers is shown in Fig. 12E, but the engineer's vice in Fig. 13 has many advantages over the wood type, especially if of the swivelling type. It can be revolved, enabling all parts of the work to be reached easily. The metal jaws should be covered with thick felt so that there is no danger of the wood being bruised.

Knives. These are not widely used by the carver, though some workers prefer them for such work as chip carving. A group of them is shown in Fig. 14.

Oilstones, slips, and grindstones. A fine stone is essential for the really sharp edge needed on carving tools. Easily the stone giving the best edge is the Arkansas. It is obtainable in flat shapes or in slips of varying sections. If a slip is not of the section needed it can be rubbed down on a flat stone using carborundum powder and oil as an abrasive. Some of the sections available are given in Fig. 15. Next in fineness is the Washita stone, followed by fine grade synthetic stones. Do not attempt to finish carving tools with a coarse stone, though it may be useful to rub down a tool which has been gashed.

When a tool needs grinding a wet grindstone (as distinct from the dry wheel) should be used. It can be either hand driven, treadle, or powered. The water in which it runs keeps the tool cool and prevents the temper from being drawn. An example is given in Fig. 16.

Strops. These are needed to remove the burr from a tool after sharpening and to give a superfine edge. Any piece of soft, pliable leather can be used if

17

Fig. 15 Oilstone slips of various shapes and sections.

Fig. 16 Grindstone. The wet type running in water should be used as there is no danger of drawing the temper of the tool.

dressed with crocus powder and Russian tallow. It can be used as it is laid flat on the bench for the outer bevel, or folded for the inner bevel. Alternatively it can be glued to a flat board or to shaped pieces of wood. The shaped pieces can be pushed across the inner bevel much as a stone slip is used, but of course must only be moved across, away from the edge, never towards it.

Bench. A rigid bench is essential. It must have a thick hardwood top so that it will withstand mallet blows without causing the work to bounce. If there is a wide top rail to the underframing the top should overhang about 37mm. to enable G cramps to be applied at the edge. For serious work a thickness of about 37mm. is the minimum, though a great deal of good work has been turned out on a thinner top. The height is largely a matter of personal stature, but about ·84m. is a good average. Lengths and widths are governed by the space available. Holes should be bored through the top large enough to take the woodcarver's bench screw and holdfast (see Fig. 12).

A carver's stand of about 76cm. height is useful for some classes of work, notably carving in the round, such as figures, busts, etc. It should be heavily built so that it will withstand mallet blows without being knocked sideways, and the top should have a hole in it to take either the wood carver's screw or the bolt of the carver's vice. Most stands have three legs so that they will stand without rocking in any position.

Chapter two

Sharpening the tools

It is impossible to do good carving unless the tools are really sharp. The relatively coarse edge given to a carpenter's chisel is not good enough for carving—in fact the condition must be more akin to that of a razor.

When tools are first obtained the edges are ground, but need to be finished on an oilstone to make them really keen. There is more in this, however, than in sharpening an ordinary woodwork chisel. It takes quite a long time to put a carving tool into really good working condition, and it is for this reason that the second-hand tools from a professional carver are sought after.

The chief reason why carving tools call for so much attention is that gouges are bevelled on the inside as well as the outside (see Fig. 1). Furthermore some carvers take off the heel of the outer bevel as it enables the tool to pass more easily around hollow curves, and in addition the corners of the heel are frequently taken off, especially on tools

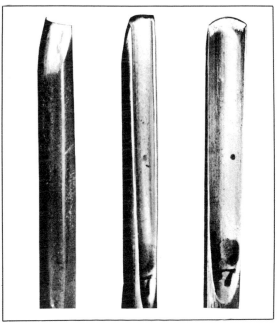

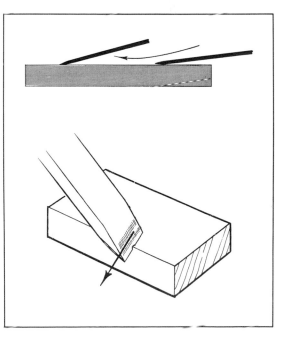

Fig. 1 Three views of gouge showing outer and inner bevels. It will be noted that the bevels are often rounded, rather than flat. The inner bevel is about one-quarter or one-third the depth of the outer one.

Fig. 2 *(top)* Sharpening rounded bevel of chisel. Note that only the heel of the bevel is rubbed down.

Fig. 3 *(below)* Removing burr.

reserved for a special purpose. However both these details are a matter of individual preference. Many sharpen a flat bevel at the outside.

So far as the inside bevel is concerned, it is clear that this increases the cutting circle, enabling the tool to be pushed easily along the hollow it has cut, especially an acute gouge. It is obvious that the heel of the bevel is of greater diameter than the edge, but by giving an inner bevel the difference is reduced. Another point is that the gouge has sometimes to be used with the hollow side downwards, and without the inner bevel, the tool would have to be held with the handle flat on the surface of the wood, an impossible position. The inner bevel enables the tool to be held at a reasonable cutting angle, and gives a natural lift to the tool as it is pushed along, avoiding digging in. This rubbing at the inside is sometimes known as 'opening the mouth'.

An exception to this is in the case of carvers whose work is entirely in soft pine. These men keep the inside of the gouge flat, with the result that a beautifully thin edge is formed which is ideal for softwood. If used on hardwood, however, the edge would be liable to crumble and break off.

Chisels. These differ from an ordinary woodworking tool as both sides are bevelled, and the bevels are kept flat though some carvers round over the heel. If the heel is removed the tool should be given a rocking movement as shown in Fig. 2. It should be realised that this rounding has only the effect of removing the heel; it should not increase the cutting angle of the tool. Only a fine-grade stone should be used—unless the edge has been gashed, in which case the bulk can be rubbed down on a coarse stone, and the edge finished off on a fine stone. This is followed by stropping on a piece of leather dressed with crocus powder mixed with Russian tallow. This gives a superfine edge, burnishes the bevel, and gets rid of the burr set up by the oilstone. If, however, the chisel has had to be rubbed down considerably, the burr may be too big to be got rid of in this way, and the best plan then is to draw the edge across a piece of softwood a couple of times as in Fig. 3. This will take off the burr completely, after which the edge can be finished by stropping both sides.

A further refinement in sharpening is to take off the square corners at one side Fig. 4B. It is of special value when working into an acute corner. For

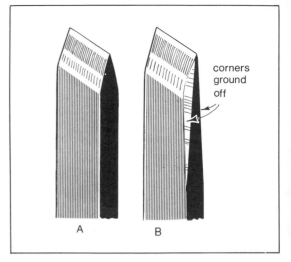

Fig. 4 Corners ground from one side of chisel.

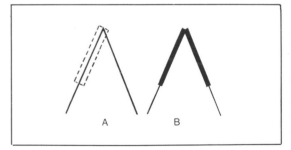

Fig. 5 How thick chisel is liable to spread wood at acute corner.

instance, in the diamond shape in Fig. 5, it is clear that if the tool is pressed straight down it will spread at the side owing to its wedge form. If, however, the square corners are rubbed down as in Fig. 4B, there is little spreading owing to the thin edge. There is no need to treat both sides alike—in fact it is better to retain the square corners at the other side as it gives a stronger edge, more suitable when the mallet has to be used. Fig. 6 shows a chisel sharpened in this way.

The skew chisel is sharpened in much the same way as the square type, except that it is at an angle. Some carvers rub down the edges at the acute

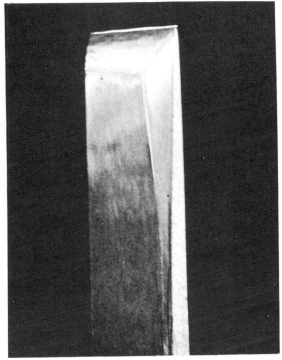

Fig. 6 How the woodcarver's chisel is sharpened. Note the rounded bevel (both sides are bevelled). A further refinement is that the thickness is ground away at one side, enabling the tool to enter an acute corner.

corner as in Fig. 7B, as here again it enables the tool to reach into an acute angle without compressing the wood at each side.

Gouges. The outer bevel has to be honed first, and this is done as shown in Fig. 8. The tool is at right angles with the stone, and is worked back and forth with a rocking movement as shown diagrammatically in Fig. 9A. In this way every part of the edge is rubbed. Take care not to overdo the rocking movement as this will take off the corners as shown by the arrow, Fig. 10, a bad fault. Some carvers prefer to rub the gouge to and fro along the whole length of the stone in an elongated figure of eight.

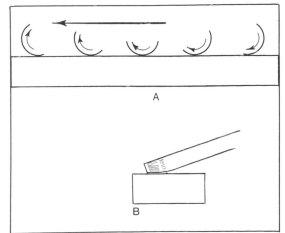

Fig. 8 Sharpening outer bevel on oilstone.

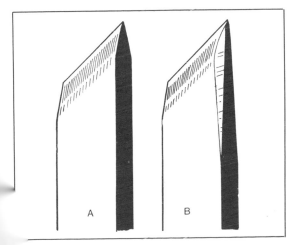

7 Sharpening the corner chisel.

Fig. 9 Diagrammatic view of gouge being honed.

It will be realised that sharpening in this way will retain the flat bevel. If the heel of the bevel is to be taken off, the handle can be lowered and the tool given a few rubs.

The inside bevel is rubbed with an oilstone slip of suitable curvature as in Fig. 11. The curvature of the slip should exactly fit the inside of the gouge. If not, make it so by rubbing to shape on a piece of Yorkstone or grindstone. Improvisation invariably brings off the corners if the slip is too flat, or the middle becomes low if it is too round.

Usually it is convenient to hold the gouge stationary and rub the slip across it, but if you prefer to work the other way round it will come to the same thing. This inner bevel should be rounded, and this is done by varying the angle of the slip as in Fig. 12. It will take a long time to produce a good inner bevel, but it is well worth it in giving smooth and easy cutting.

Another refinement used by some carvers is to rub down the edges at each side as shown in Fig. 13C. Again it enables the tool to reach into acute corners easily, but take care not to let the rubbed-down area reach to the actual corner of the edge, as this would round the latter over. However, not all carvers do this; some just treat one or two special spade gouges in this way.

Stropping. Stropping follows. For the outer bevel the tool is used with a rocking movement so that every part of the edge is reached. It is drawn across the strop so that the edge trails at an angle and does not cut into the strop, Fig. 14. For the inner bevel either the leather can be creased to form a radius that will agree with the curve of the tool, as in Fig. 15, or special strops can be made as in Fig. 16. Blocks of wood are planed to convenient sections, leather glued to them, and dressed with crocus powder and tallow as before, Fig. 17. The gouge is held against the edge of the bench, and the strop pushed across at the bevel angle. Never draw it back as the edge would cut into the leather. These special strops are not essential, however. All strops should be kept covered up when not in use to avoid picking up dust, etc.

Special tools. All the specially shaped tools, curved, front bent, back bent, and so on, are sharpened in much the same way as the more

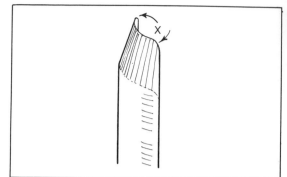

Fig. 10 Fault in gouge: corners are rounded.

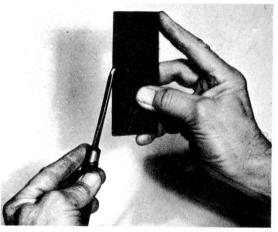

Fig. 11 Honing inner bevel.

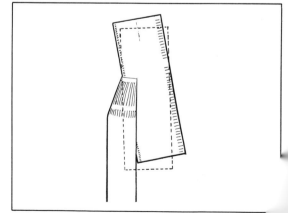

Fig. 12 Honing inside bevel.

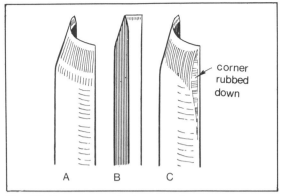

Fig. 13 How gouge is sharpened.

A   B   C

corner
rubbed
down

general tools. The only ones slightly awkward are front bent gouges and the spoon bits or entering chisels. The reason for this is that the oilstone slip tends to foul the cranked shape of the tool, so that only the end of the slip can be used, as in Fig. 18. However, there is no real difficulty.

Once tools are in good condition they need little more than stropping to keep them keen. Eventually the edge needs to be restored with oilstone and slip, but the secret is never to let the tools become in bad condition. On this score make a roll for them as soon as they are obtained, and never let them be bunched together in a heap. Note from Fig. 23 that the tool pockets are not opposite each other but are staggered. In this way the tools do not foul each other.

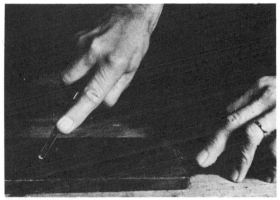

Fig. 14 Stropping outer bevel. Tool is given a rocking movement.

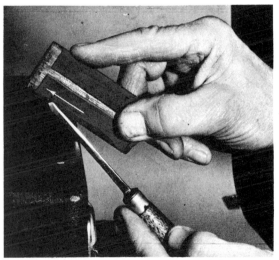

Fig. 16 Alternative method using special strop.

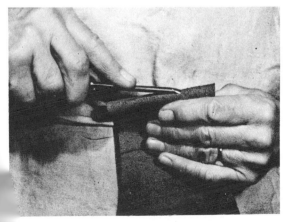

. **15** Stropping inner bevel on leather.

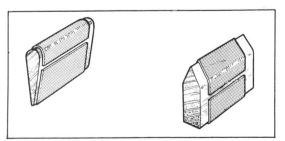

Fig. 17 Leather-covered strops for finishing gouges and parting tools. Many carvers use only a strip of leather creased up to follow the curve.

23

If a tool is gashed or the edge becomes uneven it should be held at right angles to the stone and rubbed until the gash is entirely removed, or until every part of the unevenness has been touched. This will show as a line of light, as in Fig. 19, and the parts of the bevel to be rubbed are obvious. Unless this is done the unevenness becomes perpetuated.

The parting tool. Although apparently nothing more than two chisels joined together at an angle, the sharpening is somewhat tricky, especially in the smaller sizes. The tool is sharpened with outer bevels slightly rounded as in chisels and gouges, and with a smaller inner bevel formed with a triangular oilstone slip, Fig. 20. The consequence of this is that the internal angle, instead of being really sharp, becomes rounded owing to the slip losing its sharp corner (Fig. 21), with the result that a hook shape is formed as at Fig. 21B owing to the outer bevels being straight and meeting at a sharp angle. The hook becomes more pronounced or a hollow may be formed as in Fig. 22 if one bevel is rubbed more than the other.

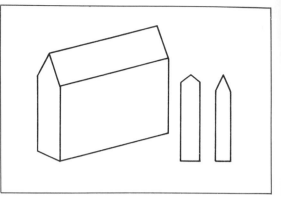

Fig. 20 Slips for sharpening inside of parting tool.

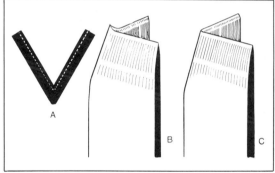

Fig. 21 Method of sharpening parting tool:
A Section showing edge in dotted lines: B Hook formed at apex of edges: C Corner rubbed down to remove hook.

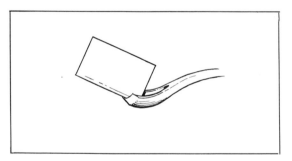

Fig. 18 Sharpening the front bent gouge.

line of light

Fig. 19 End of unevenly sharpened gouge ground flat.

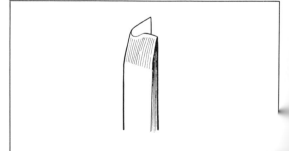

Fig. 22 Unevenly sharpened parting tool.

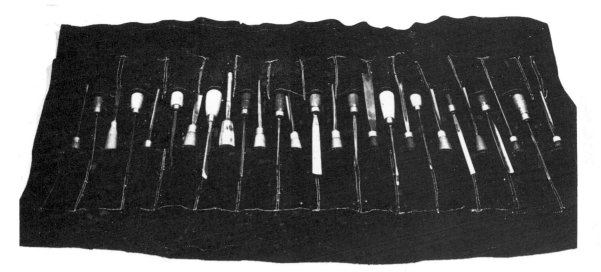

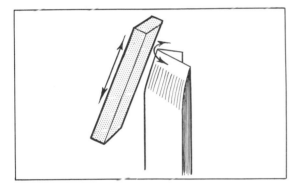

Fig. 23 Useful roll to hold 28 tools. This can be made in baize or canvas. Note that the two rows are staggered so that the tools clear each other.

Fig. 24 *(left)* Sharp corner of parting tool taken off.

Fig. 25 Detail of mace in mahogany and silver. Carved by William Wheeler.

The extreme point of the hook is not sharp because of the thickness necessarily left between the rounded inner angle and the sharp outer corner. This is corrected by slightly rounding over the outer corner so that it conforms with the inner rounded angle. This is shown at Fig. 21C. This has a second advantage in that the slight rounding of the outer corner makes the tool easier to manipulate as it is less liable to drift. Fig. 24 shows the corner being rounded. The actual rounding is so small that the appearance in the cut is practically that of a square, sharp corner.

Those who use the parting tool for really large lettering will find it essential to sharpen rounded bevels at the outside rather than straight ones, because otherwise it is extremely difficult or impossible to negotiate curved members.

Chapter three

Handling
the tools

Almost without exception carving tools are held in both hands. The skilled carver is usually ambidextrous, the advantage being that it often enables the direction of the cut to be altered to suit the grain without shifting the position of the wood. In this chapter we talk about right-hand working, but it should be understood that left-hand carving is exactly the same except that the terms right and left are interchanged.

How tools are held. Fig. 1 shows how the right hand grips the handle and provides the forward pressure, whilst the left hand largely guides the tool and exerts a backward braking force which prevents over-running. These two opposing movements are not independent, but are an automatically concerted effort.

Consider the probable result of using forward pressure only with one hand only. It would be practically impossible to stop the tool at an exact position, because the force required to cut the wood would result in the tool over-running. When two hands are used the checking power of the left

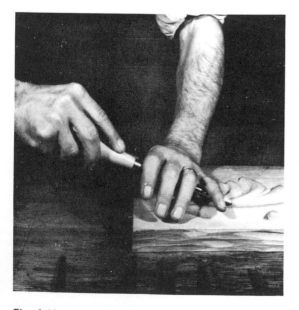

Fig. 1 How woodcarving gouge is held. In some cases the fingers of the left hand curl right round the blade. The purpose is to act as a guiding and restraining force. Note how the ball of the hand rests on the work.

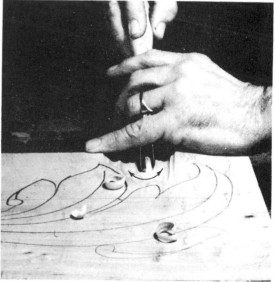

Fig. 2 How gouge can be given a slicing action. Note that this applies only to gouges, not to veiners or parting tools. It eases the cut, and is often effective on tricky grain.

hand prevents this. With practice the combined movement of the two hands becomes automatic.

In most cases the ball of the left hand rests on the wood, and becomes a sort of pivot upon which all movement is made. Generally this anchor is not shifted during a cut, the hand remaining stationary on the wood and the movement of the gouge controlled by contraction of the fingers. All this becomes obvious after half-an-hour of practice with tools.

When a gouge is of semi-circular shape it sometimes helps to give it a rocking movement so that it has a slicing cut as in Fig 2. Any gouge, the shape of which is part of a circle, can be used in this way, but clearly it is impossible for a tool of U shape. To attempt to use this with a rocking movement would only result in the flat sides tearing the wood. This is made clear in Fig. 3 which shows that whereas the tool of semi-circular form Fig. 3A slips round the curve of its own making, the U form Fig. 3B cannot slide without forcing away the wood. The same thing applies to the V tool which must move forward only without rocking.

Generally it is easier to cut across the grain than with it, and consequently the roughing in should be done across the grain when feasible providing the tool is really sharp. Quite apart from ease in cutting, the tool is more readily controlled because there is no tendency for it to follow the grain as in the case of working *with* the grain.

Difficult grain. The question of grain needs to be reckoned with in carving. Often enough the direction in which the tool should be taken is obvious, but when using a semi-circular gouge it should be realised that two directions of grain have to be reckoned with; up-and-down, and side-to-side. The reason is that, owing to the semi-circular shape of the tool, the cut is at the side as well as at the bottom. Some of these problems are made clear in Fig. 4. At Fig. 4A it is clear that the tool should be taken in the straight forward direction so far as up-and-down direction of the grain is concerned. At Fig. 4B the tool is liable to tear out at one side although leaving a smooth finish at the other. A difficult case is that at Fig. 4C where, if the tool is taken in the direction shown by the arrow, it will leave a smooth finish at the bottom of the hollow, but will tear out at the side marked by the arrow.

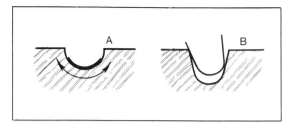

Fig. 3 Why veiner must not be rocked. The gouge (A) can be given a slicing movement, easing the cut and helping on tricky grain. This cannot be done with the veiner (B) owing to the U shape.

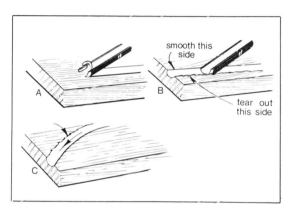

Fig. 4 How direction of grain affects use of tool. The grain at both the surface and at the edge has to be considered.

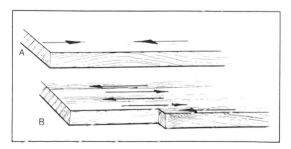

Fig. 5 A Undulating grain affecting direction of cut: B Streaked grain, specially difficult for carving.

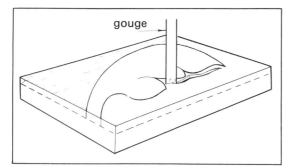

gouge

Fig. 6 Setting-in around outline of design. This may not be practicable in dense hardwood (see below).

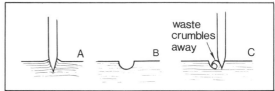

A   B   waste crumbles away   C

Fig. 7 How setting-in in hardwood can be simplified: **A** Tool liable to be forced into design outline, or tool apt to fracture: **B** Preliminary gouge cut on waste side: **C** Waste crumbles at outside into gouge cut.

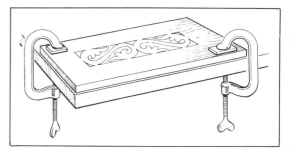

Fig. 8 Work held down with G cramps.

Some woods are more difficult than others, because of undulating grain, as at Fig. 5A in which the tool would have to be taken in opposite directions in different parts of the wood. Still more awkward is when the grain runs in streaks side by side at an angle as at Fig. 5B. In a broad cut the tool might easily be working both *with* and *against* the grain in different parts of its edge. Such woods are not suitable for carving. When they *must* be used a really keen edge and thin cut is the answer, plus a great deal of patience in working in the direction which gives best results.

Setting-in. Most designs at some stage in the carving require setting-in. In this the outline is cut in with gouges and chisels which approximate to the particular part of the curve. With softwood there is no difficulty as the wood gives under the wedge pressure of the tool. The only essential is to make the initial cut slightly to the waste side of the line, as otherwise the wedge action will force the tool beyond the line.

An example of setting-in is given in Fig. 6 in which the centre leafwork is to remain standing up and the background cut back. Chisel cuts are made all round, these following the outline approximately, but ignoring small detail and leaving a mass of wood sufficiently big to enable the detail to be carved. Afterwards the surrounding waste is cut away with a fairly big semi-circular gouge.

When a hardwood is being carved this method is often impracticable, because the resistance to the

entry of the tool is too great. Consider what is happening. The substance of the gouge is perhaps 3mm. ($\frac{1}{8}$in.) thick, and, if the tool is driven in to the full extent of its bevel, the wood has necessarily to be displaced by this amount. Usually this cannot be done with hardwood, or, if it is attempted, may easily result in the tool splintering near the edge. For work of this kind the only plan is to go around the outline of the design with a U tool, using this on the waste side. The U tool is more convenient than a semi-circular gouge because it can be sunk in deeper without the top corners digging beneath the surface of the wood. The purpose of this pre-liminary work is to free the wood to the waste side of the outline so that when setting-in follows, the thin lip of waste wood crumbles away and the resistance is largely reduced. Fig. 7 shows this idea.

For the majority of work the gouge can be used with hand pressure, or helped with blows from the ball of the hand. Sometimes, however, the mallet is needed, especially in the preliminary bosting-in stages of carving in the round, or in setting-in. The professional carver usually has at least two mallets of varying weights, and he uses the lighter whenever practicable because continuous use of t mallet can be a most tiring task, and the movement of an unnecessarily heavy tool is wasted effort.

In a flat design in which the background has to be lowered equally all over, a small router is a most useful tool. It is not used for removing the bulk of the waste (this is done with normal carving tools), but rather to bring recesses already made to equal depth. Thus in the preliminary grounding out the depth is kept slightly less than the finished size, and the router used to make the whole equal. This will leave a more or less smooth surface, and it is usual to finish off with a flat gouge so that the tool marks characteristic of carving are retained.

Fixing wood when carving

It is essential that the wood is firmly anchored so that both hands are free to handle the tool. The method of gripping depends upon the form of the work.

G Cramps. When a flat panel is being carved it can be held down flat on the bench with ordinary G cramps providing that the work is large enough for the cramps to be fixed in positions where they will not interfere with the movement of the hands. Thus a large panel can easily be held as in Fig. 8. Similarly a long rail could be so fixed without the cramps being in the way.

Buttons. It will be realised, however, that when a small panel is being carved the projection of the cramps would be a nuisance, and a simple alternative is to use small wood buttons as in Fig. 9A. These are screwed to the bench, and can be notched so that there is a minimum projection.

A still simpler way, which saves notching the buttons, is to use thin strips which rest at one end on the work and at the other on waste blocks of the same thickness. Screws driven into the bench hold the whole firmly Fig. 9B.

Thin wood. For thin wood the buttons at Fig. 9C can be used. They are not rebated—there is not enough thickness—but the one end is tapered so that at the tip fits over the wood, and the projection is negligible. Yet another method in which there is no

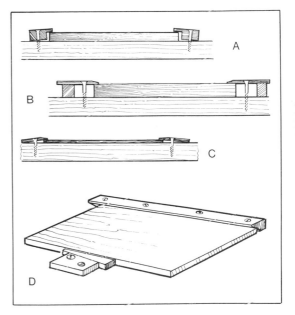

Fig. 9 Various methods of holding panels, etc. These leave the surface largely clear so that the movement of the hands is not restricted.

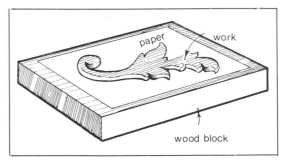

Fig. 10 How small parts can be held.

projection at all at one side, is that at Fig. 9D. A bevelled piece of wood is screwed to the bench and the work slipped beneath the bevel. A thin wood block is screwed into the bench about 12mm ($\frac{1}{2}$in.) away from the free edge of the wood, and a wedge tapped in, so gripping the work.

Sometimes the work is of an odd shape or is so fragile or thin that none of the foregoing would be practicable. An example is the small type of applied decoration sometimes seen in Chippendale and Adam woodwork. Such parts may be only 6mm.

29

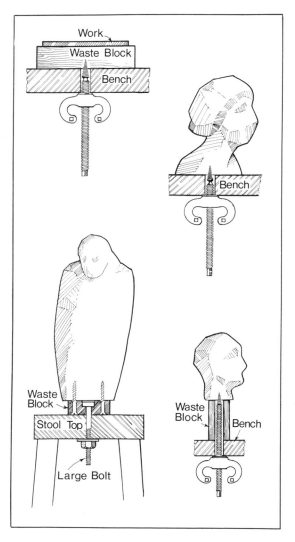

thick, and the outline has to be fretted before carving can begin. The simplest way is to glue the fretted shape to a thicker block with a piece of newspaper interposed as in Fig. 10. Thin glue should be used, enabling the work to be prised away with a thin table knife after carving. The paper separates in its thickness so that it lifts easily although being held securely enough during carving. The block is held to the bench either with cramps or, preferably, with a wood carver's bench screw. Fig. 11 shows the idea.

Woodcarver's bench screw. The great advantage of the carver's screw is that there are no projecting cramps in the way of the hands, but it does mean that a fairly big hole has to be bored in either the work or in a waste block to which the work is temporarily glued. Thus in Fig. 12 the screw enters the base of the wood where it is not seen, whereas in Fig. 11, in which the work would be too thin to take the screw, it enters a thick waste block.

It will be realised that for such work as that in Fig. 12, although it would be easy enough to carve the top part, the lower portion would be difficult since the bench would be in the way of both the hands and the tools. It is therefore desirable to raise up the work, and a simple way is to bore a hole through a waste block of wood and put this beneath the work as in Fig. 14. Here the whole thing can be reached without difficulty, and it can be turned round at any angle by slackening the screw.

Vices. The ordinary bench vice as fixed to a carpenter's bench is not really suitable for carving as so much of the wood is masked by either the jaw or the bench edge. Most useful are the carver's chops which, according to type, can either be fixed to the bench with its attached cramps, or be held down by a large bolt which passes downwards through a hole in the bench. The jaws of the vice should be lined with leather so that danger of bruising the work is minimised. Still better is the swivelling metal-worker's vice, the base of which is bolted to the bench. It can be revolved through any angle to enable any part of the work to be reached easily. It is shown in Fig. 15. Here again the jaws need to be lined.

Carver's stand. For large figure work in th⟨e⟩ round it is necessary to be able to walk round th⟨e⟩

Fig. 11 *(top left)* Carver's bench screw fixed to waste block.

Fig. 12 *(top right)* Bust held down with carver's bench screw.

Fig. 13 *(bottom left)* How large work can be fixed.

Fig. 14 *(bottom right)* Holding work clear of bench.

Fig. 15 Engineer's vice with swivelling head

Fig. 16 Carving in the round, work fixed in chops held on carver's stand.

wood easily so that all aspects can be noted. This means that fixing the work to the bench is of little value. Much the better idea is to use the carver's stand which has a substantial top with central hole through which a bolt can be passed. It should be heavily made so that it will withstand mallet blows. The carver can easily walk round and view work fixed to this.

There are various ways of fixing the work. When not too heavy the carver's screw can be used, but if too big for this, a waste block can be used. This has a centre hole through which a large bolt can be passed, and is screwed to the bottom of the work as in Fig. 13.

Chapter four

Drawing and design

Drawing is the basis of all good craftsmanship. On it depends quality, and without it its true and exalted purpose is missed. Toolmanship is not enough; neither is drawing and design; rather it is the combination of both which produces the highest result. This has always been true whatever the craft. It provides that quality which gives pleasure for all time, more particularly if its purpose is functional.

Although the purpose of this book is for the most part to provide a practical approach to the craft of woodcarving, it will fail in its purpose if drawing and design are found wanting in any stage. With this in mind the creative faculties must be trained through drawing. Methods and systems for this training are numerous, but, providing they are not rigid and divorced from a particular material, one can accept most of them.

Fundamentally the method chosen should be for the most part experimental and initially adventuresome. Furthermore, it should be allied to some specific art or craft, running parallel as it were with the materials and tools involved. If you can appreciate, too, that any talent which you possess, or hope to possess or improve upon is multiplied by the gift of memory, it will not be difficult to under-

Motifs for wood carving taken from nature.

stand that a basic form of training in drawing is vital. Time and time again students and apprentices have complained that they can cut wood or stone with good results, but cannot draw or design. It is extremely difficult to convey to them with understanding that their work has missed its appeal through lack of drawing.

How then must one set about improving one's drawing? The following suggestions have been found invaluable in assisting would-be carvers. As memory is stored observation one must keep it well stocked, replenishing it from time to time, not only by studying all the magnificent work of the past but also what is best in contemporary work. With the knowledge gained, one can add to this heritage and make one's contribution to tradition.

A sketch book. The first advice is to keep a sketch book. Fill it with drawings that interest you, not necessarily only with period pieces of carved work—though this is important—but with items which make an appeal by virtue of the age in which we live. Even instruments of a scientific nature, and all the wonderful shapes they help to produce in their many ramifications, are worth noting. Try expressing the line of movement seen in sporting activities or animal and plant life, so increasing the range of material for your sketch book. Costume is well worth recording, particularly if it is associated with today's activities; a motor cyclist's outfit, or a surgeon ready for the theatre. I recently had to carve aircraft for an heraldic achievement, and was also asked to carve crocodiles for a similar purpose.

There is endless scope, but items must be recorded in your sketch book when seen. I have inspected sketch books of young students submitted for examination purposes, and have been able to see their interest in a particular field of study, and, in many cases, deep research. Then there is the abundance of traditional work in museums, churches, etc. Make a note in pencil, analyse it, draw sections of it, note in writing the material from which it was carved, also the finish. If the work is gilt, examine it closely in the light of the chapter given on that subject (see page 115) and investigate whether it is burnished or matt, whether the ground is gesso or paint. Has the gesso been built up heavily and the gesso carved, not the wood, as in the case of those beautiful table tops of the Georgian period? Note when your sketches were

Fig. 2

done, for the date gives interest later.

Everything sketched may not necessarily be good in design and workmanship. That is not the point. The whole purpose of the exercise in keeping a sketch book is to stimulate your interest, train your inventive faculties, and express yourself freely with a pencil. Your sketch book will be a rich store of information and will help in subject matter in designing, whether it has to be in the traditional stream, or something individual.

Drawing from nature. At this point one should stress the importance of life drawing, and the careful study of plant form. Bearing in mind again the purpose of this book, the drawing of plant form should be more advantageous for gaining experience and interest in designing and practising wood carving. If you want to design and carve ornament successfully, appreciate the difference between a good line and a bad one, and understand form at its best, you must draw from nature. Throughout the centuries this has been the basis of ornament, be it treated naturalistically like the screen work on mediaeval carving or the much more conventional or sophisticated stuff of the Renaissance period, which comes under the broad heading of acanthus foliage. What a wealth of interest and design for all to study!

History, too, would be poorer without ornament, for fragments found all over the world are a great source of information in establishing accuracy in dates for historians.

So far as wood is concerned, ornament well done adds interest to construction. On the other hand, a good deal of it found on furniture of today certainly does not add interest or in the slightest degree enhance it.

Drawing practice. Now to practice with pencil and paper. Choose what you will in plant life, but consider before final selection whether the flower, fruit, and foliage could be translated to wood without losing its characteristics. In your sketches make them full size, and let them be diagrammatic rather than pictorial. Block out with single lines main shapes first as one would do in carving, and let shading and shadows give the sections one could follow when carving. More often than not they indicate the relief and therefore the thickness of material.

It is interesting before leaving the drawing to make simple designs of motifs suggested by nature on the same sheet of paper, and whilst the plant or spray of foliage is before you, draw sections at various points. This will enable you to tackle a job in wood with assurance, and bost it in with boldness and spontaneity rather than use sporadic cutting, which always produces some form of disunity in the final finish, and if analysed is usually brought about through lack of interpretation of the subject. The illustrations in Figs. 1, 2 and 3 are freely adapted studies of plant forms for use in designing woodcarving and help to illustrate the importance of knowing the subject before carving it.

Heraldry. In this connection the study and drawing of heraldry adds a wonderful interest to carving. It adds scope and adventure in colour and gives practice in gesso and gilding, the principles of which are explained in Chapter 19. Heraldry is a grand subject for all craftsmen to study, and in particular the carver in wood. Heraldry, too, is a science as well as an art. As far as the former is

Fig. 3

concerned this was all complete by the 13th century, with its classification and nomenclature clearly stated in every patent of arms. It is not complicated, everything has a name, and although the names are many, all are explained in sketches in textbooks on the subject. The colours are limited to five, Red, Blue, Green, Black, Purple, and the metals two, Gold or Silver, whatever the blazon.

Whether it is to be a fine work or not depends entirely on the interpretation given by the craftsman in the particular material he is associated with, in our case wood. Here again good drawing and design are the criteria. The artist's licence given to craftsmen in the making up of heraldic achievements is manifold, providing one keeps to the book of rules (the science).

Now for practice. Try to procure a good rendering of a coat of arms, in colour preferably. Draw it thoroughly, and assume you are going to carve it in wood, as we did the plant forms. This will give an objective and interest. Remember in doing so (a) that the proportion of, say, shield to helm and mantling to crest is sound, and a good standard to work to in original work; (b) the shape of a shield is an arbitrary one, and the artist is given freedom to introduce what shape he likes, providing proportion, fitness for purpose, and materials are taken into consideration; (c) as the whole will be coloured, the charges on the shield need only be carved slightly in relief and the drawing of them be bold, simple in outline, and fully occupying the shape, even if they appear exaggerated or simple like the example on page 48 (heraldic lion exercise); (d) the mantling, helm, and crest should for the most part make good use of the whole thickness of the material. The study of good examples will show what is meant. Having learnt the elements from books plus the experience gained from this exercise, try an original design based on a surname, profession, or trade, or a combination of all. This is called a rebus in heraldic language, and as early as the thirteenth century and even today forms a basis on which to produce an heraldic achievement. There are innumerable examples, both in ecclesiastical and secular works, and they can be an incentive to keep on designing and drawing.

ouldings. In this chapter dealing with mould- s the examples given are based on traditional

examples, so the practical approach to cutting can be quickly achieved. Here again is another opportunity for drawing and design. Refer to the sections illustrated on page 65. Redraw them on a sheet of paper, and then design some original patterns as well as the best of traditional work. This will at least introduce you to the simplest form of design, i.e., repetition, then as practice continues proportion, composition, beauty of line, will fall into their places, more so if they are associated with tools for a particular craft and a definite purpose. This is expressed in a wonderful way by W. R. Lethaby: 'Proper ornamentation may be defined as a language addressed to the eye; it is a pleasant thought expressed in the speech of the tool.'

Crown Copyright.

Christ riding upon an ass. A late 15th century carving from South Germany in limewood.

Chapter five

Exercise in handling tools

The purpose of this exercise is to enable the beginner to learn how to handle tools, and to acquire confidence in using them. The design given in Fig. 1 is a simple piece of conventional leafwork. It does not represent any particular style, and has no special purpose of its own beyond being a simple motif of decoration. If the result does not turn out exactly as in the photograph it does not matter in the slightest—in fact it is all to the good if you work out your own ideas on the general form and modelling. The great thing is to adopt long sweeping strokes which follow the natural flow of the leaves, at the same time taking into account the peculiarities of grain. Make a point, too, of changing hands when using the tools in the modelling. It helps much to get confidence, particularly when tackling three-dimension or turned work and jobs which cannot be moved

Fig. 1 Simple panel suitable for the beginner. This gives good practice in grounding, setting-in, and elementary modelling.

easily once they are fixed to the bench, or when working *in situ* where the material is permanently fixed.

The first necessity is to put the design on the wood, and one way is to make an enlargement of the design in Fig. 2 by drawing a series of squares on paper, and transferring the design map fashion. Do not be satisfied with simply regarding the whole as a series of lines which intersect with the squares at certain points, but rather use them just as a guide or invisible instructor to get you going. Later this way can be varied or dropped, and other methods employed with which you may be more familiar.

Those who prefer can draw the design freehand with variations in design, providing it is remembered that this conventional form of leaf has a rhythmic growth with the lines produced by the tools all fanning out from the base of the leaf. This is different from the structure of natural foliage, where subsidiary veins always spring or radiate from the centre vein of the leaf. If it is not exactly like that in Fig. 1 it does not matter providing the lines are harmonious and flowing.

Transferring the design. This design on paper can be transferred to the wood by means of carbon paper, care being taken not to shift the paper during the operation. The simplest way is to fold the paper over the edges of the wood. Avoid using drawing-pins where possible, for sometimes the holes left behind give an unsightly appearance, even if they are subsequently filled. Sellotape is excellent for holding the paper to the wood. The ideal wood to use for the exercise is lime, but any clean piece of softwood will do. First-quality yellow pine does well, or the softer hardwoods—walnut, Honduras mahogany, agba, pear, etc.

Fig. 2 The design drawn out in 25mm. (1in.) squares. This can be reproduced on paper in full size by drawing in a grid of 1in. squares, and plotting the design map fashion.

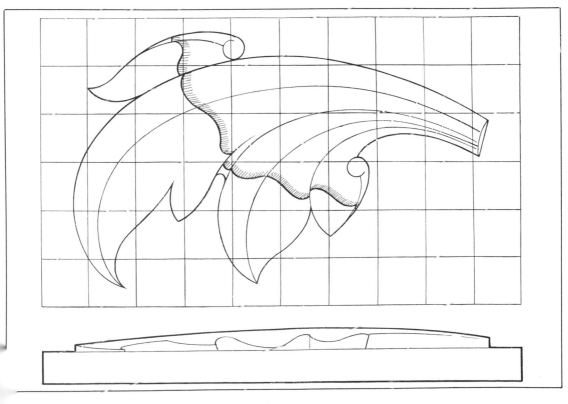

Grounding in. The wood first to be removed is termed the groundwork, and to achieve this set a marking gauge to the depth 11mm. ($\frac{1}{2}$in.) and mark round the edges. Use a fairly large gouge of semi-circular section for the bulk of the work (say No. 9, 13mm. ($\frac{1}{2}$in.) or 19mm. ($\frac{3}{4}$in.)), and, working in from the edges, cut away the groundwork to within about 1mm. ($\frac{1}{16}$in.) of the finished depth. For a start let the gouge run out to the surface as the outline is approached, as in Fig. 3, and work across the grain as far as possible as the wood is less likely to tear out. It is also a good way of seeing whether your tools are really sharp when working across grain. If preferred the mallet can be used, the main criterion being whether the material is tough.

Fig. 3 First stage in grounding

Now work round the main outline with the gouge as in Fig. 4, keeping about 1·5mm. ($\frac{1}{16}$in.) or 3mm. ($\frac{1}{8}$in.) outside the line and only approximately to the shape, omitting all smaller detail as shown. The idea is to lessen the resistance when the next stage of setting-in is being done. In this a fairly flat gouge is taken about 1·5mm. ($\frac{1}{16}$in.) from the outline as in Fig. 5. Again omit detail but follow the outline reasonably closely. It will be found that the wood will crumble away easily on the waste side as at Fig. 4B, owing to the gouge cuts already made

Fig. 4 Second stage in grounding. The gouge cut approximately to the outline (**A**) enables the wood to crumble away easily on the waste side when setting-in is done (**B**).

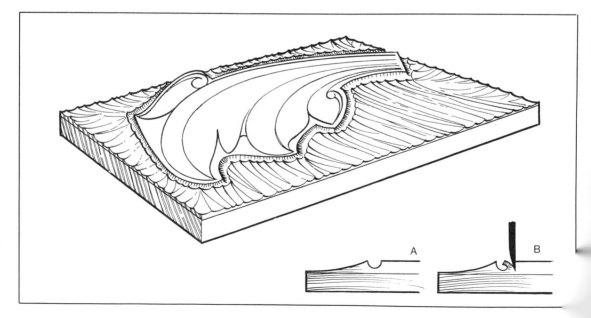

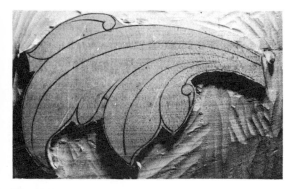

Fig. 5 Groundwork cut away.

Fig. 7 The panel partly modelled

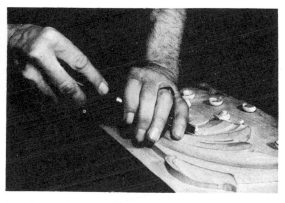

Fig. 6 Bosting-in with the gouge.

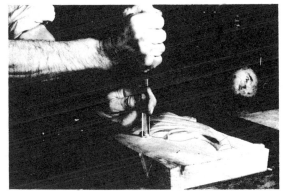

Fig. 8 Setting-in with gouge.

around the shape. Take care not to chop in more deeply than the background depth. The groundwork can now be cut away with the half-round gouge right up to the outline of the design.

To complete this grounding-out stage go round the outline once again, setting-in right up to the line, and selecting gouges which approximate to the particular curve being cut. Again be careful to avoid chopping in too deeply. To make the groundwork as flat as possible use a nearly flat, wide gouge, such as a No. 3, 19mm. ($\frac{3}{4}$in.) or 25mm. (1in.). Keep the corners free from digging in, and work right up to the design. A straight-edge placed over the groundwork will reveal whether the surface is reasonably flat.

grounding is excellent practice in handling the s. The result must be reasonably flat, but do not

attempt to remove all tool marks. The grounded surface in this particular case is for the most part finished off with flat carving chisels of varying sizes. Grounders, too, can be used in small areas not easily accessible to the chisels. If the marks left by the tools give interest let them remain. However, it must be remembered that getting a smooth surface (with tools only) is sometimes demanded, particularly on furniture and small work. This is not so difficult as it would appear, and it is suggested that you try both methods on this exercise.

The right hand grasps the handle of the tool and supplies the forward pressure, whilst the left hand is about evenly around blade and handle and acts as a sort of resistance or brake. It is in fact the interplay of pressure between the hands that gives control. After practice this will come automatically.

Modelling. Now follows the interesting work, that of bosting- or roughing-in. It will be seen from Fig. 2 that the relief of the leafwork is not constant, but that the surface undulates, sinking down from the high parts nearly down to the level of the groundwork. A fairly wide gouge of moderate curvature is used (say a No. 8, 19mm. ($\frac{3}{4}$in.)). Work in long, even sweeps, following the direction of the main vein. Do not worry unduly about ridges between the gouge marks. The whole idea is to work in confident sweeps, making the tool follow exactly the path you want. If it tends to tear out in one direction, work the other way. Cut in the hollows first, the gouge held with the rounded side downwards, and, where it reverses into a rounded section at each side, use a fairly flat gouge with hollow side downwards.

For a first attempt you will probably find that the corners of the gouge will catch into the wood, causing grain tearing or whiskers of wood. Do not be worried by this but go over the work a second time (third or fourth if necessary), again working in long sweeps, the tool marks by their direction suggesting the natural flow of the leaf form.

It is inevitable that the grain will tear out in parts. In one long sweep it may start smoothly, only to tear out as the end is reached, or vice versa, but by working in the opposite direction it is usually possible to give a clean finish. Fig. 6 shows the bosting-in stage.

In any leafwork of this kind avoid getting a flat effect in the modelling. Rather let the whole undulate in clean, flowing form with even, natural sweeps. It helps to lift the work up to eye level and look across it when the general true shape will become obvious.

Final setting-in. It will be found that this roughing-in will have altered the outline of the design, and it will be necessary to cut in all round a second time. Lightly pencil in the required outline, and cut in with really sharp tools, slightly undercutting, and selecting gouges which approximate to the shape. Make the cuts run cleanly into those at each side, for these are the final cuts and give quality to the work. The groundwork will have to be finished up to the new line, and the necessity for not setting-in too deeply in the first place will now be obvious. Any deep or false stab marks will show as blemishes on the groundwork if care is not exercised at this stage.

Fig. 9 Conventional leafwork on turned lime roundel. Carved by Ronald Gilbert.

Fig. 10 Coat of arms in limewood, gilt and coloured. About 1.2m. (4ft.) high. Carved by Sydney Riches.

It would be a good exercise after completion of the carving to draw freehand the same design on another piece of wood. Then swiftly go over the outline with a V or parting tool only. You will be surprised what assurance and confidence it will give you, in drawing and handling of tools; and incidentally it is another way of seeing what degree of sharpness your parting tool has, for it will have to cope with grain from many directions.

Chapter six

In many respects this is the simplest form of carving. There is no attempt at modelling of any kind, the effect being obtained purely by single cuts with gouge or chisel. At the same time it calls for neatness and clean cutting. It can be extremely effective, especially when used as a repeat or variegated pattern, and was widely used during the oak period of furniture making. It is closely allied to chip carving where the effect is also obtained in the simplest way by making cuts which meet in the thickness of the wood, so allowing the chip to come away easily and cleanly. This last point is in fact the chief feature of carving. No

Fig. 2 Board with gouge and chisel cuts. Except for slight rounding or hollowing of the groundwork in some cases, all the patterns are produced by simple cuts with gouge or chisel. See key to the patterns in Fig. 1.

Simple tool cuts

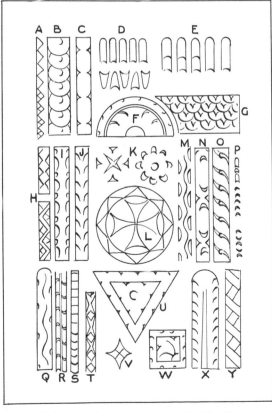

Reference key to the panel in Fig. 2.

scraping away of the waste chips should be necessary—if it is needed it is a sign that the work has not been properly done. The first incision is usually across the grain, and the second runs in to meet it, so freeing the chip. In some cases three cuts from different directions may be needed.

The panel shown in Fig. 2 consists for the greater part of simple straight cuts with gouge or chisel. In some cases it may be necessary to work a preliminary hollowing or rounding of the groundwork, but the decoration itself is done with elementary cuts. The usual plan is to cut down, generally across the grain, and then remove the chip by a sloping cut, or one which is horizontal.

Gouge cuts. The simplest form is that in Fig. 3. Only one gouge is used, and the downward cut is made as at Fig. 4A. Note that the tool slopes at a slight angle, the idea being that the surface so formed is more easily seen, whereas a vertical cut or one which is undercut leaves a thin edge and is not so effective.

In a softwood such as lime or pine the downward cut can be made with hand pressure only, as in Fig. 7, or by a thump from the open palm, but for harder woods it is necessary to use the mallet. The gouge is then entered into the wood at an angle at the required distance away, and the handle almost at once lowered so that parallel sides are cut to the shape (Fig. 4, see also Fig. 8). Make an effort to finish the cut in one movement after the work has been set down with chisel or gouge. If successful it will give a freshness to the work which is fundamental. If on the other hand your efforts are not up to expectation, try moving the bulk first, leaving only a fine cut to finish off.

When a row of such gouge cuts has to be made it is generally desirable to make all the downward or stabbing cuts first. There are two reasons for this, one being that these cuts are liable to take the edge off the tool quickly. It is therefore better to do all this work first, so that the tool can be sharpened afresh and used for the finer and more exacting work of paring away the chips.

Still more important is the fact that the downward cuts are liable to displace the fibres owing to the wedge shape of the cutting edge. It may easily happen therefore that if the adjoining chip has been

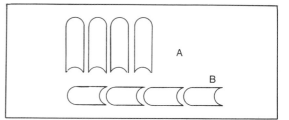

Fig. 3 Gouge cuts with parallel sides.

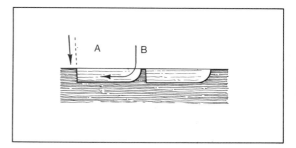

Fig. 4 (A) Shows the downward cut, and (B) Removal of waste.

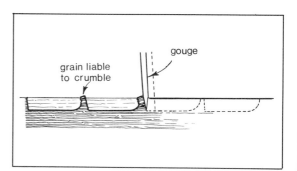

Fig. 5 Why it is desirable to make all downward cuts first.

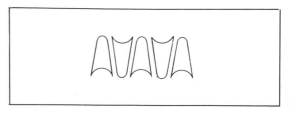

Fig. 6 Tapered sides to gouge cuts.

Fig. 7 Downward stabs being made. Figs 7 and 8 refer to D, E, P, and R shown in Figs 1 and 2.

. 8 How waste is removed with gouge.

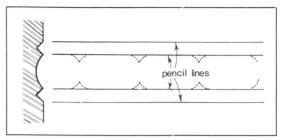

Fig. 9 Decorated channelling.

Fig. 10 Removing waste with skew chisel.

removed the wood may crumble owing to the shortness of the grain. This is shown clearly in Fig. 5. This point in fact is worth keeping in mind in all such operations. In some cases the angle at which the gouge is taken into the wood is maintained so that the sides of the cut converge rather than remain parallel. This is shown in Fig. 6. It is effective for some work, but generally parallel sides are preferable. Another variation is to leave reed shapes in part of the fluting as at Fig. 2E. To cut this, two downward stabs are made, the bottom one shallower than the other. The top flute is then taken out in the ordinary way, and the rounding of the reed completed afterwards. A chisel or flat gouge can be used for this. Other variations of the same idea are given at Fig. 2P and R. This form of decoration is specially effective if a rounded channel is worked first and the gouge cuts made in this. The pattern at Fig. 2N uses this feature, but the direction of the gouge cuts is reversed. Between the main gouge pockets are smaller cuts made similarly but with a smaller gouge.

Decorated channelling. Of a different type is the pattern at Fig. 2C. To start this the main centre hollow is worked with a fairly flat gouge, and at each side is a channel worked with the V tool. Fig. 9 shows the idea. Pencil lines are drawn in first, these marking the extent of the members. There is no need to put in the third centre line marking the bottom of the V. Simply work between the outside lines, making sure that the V tool does not stray beyond them.

The repeats are stepped out with dividers, and at each nick a downward stab is made at an angle with a gouge, a size which will fit the curve being selected. The curve it cuts must, of course, flow in an unbroken line into the straight pencil lines. The cut is taken down to the bottom of the V cut only, and it will be realised that the gouge must not be held upright, but rather at an angle, so that the outer corner of the gouge stops level with the bottom of the V. This enables the waste to be cut away with a chisel held in alignment with the outer surface as in Fig. 10. Generally a small skew chisel is the most convenient tool to use for this.

Similar is the method of cutting the pattern at Fig. 21. The hollow member is worked first, and a series of cuts is made at an angle as in Fig. 11, a large and a small gouge being used alternately. The waste is removed as in Fig. 12, a skew chisel being used and held at an angle.

Various patterns. Designs in Fig. 2A, H, K (left), L, S, T, V, and Y are all variations of chip carving, and are done in every case by downward stabs with the waste eased away by a sloping cut. L is slightly more elaborate, but the principle of cutting is the same. The centre dividing lines are cut in first and the wood sloped away at each side. Where the lines are curved a gouge is used rather than the chisel. Note how interest is gained by certain of the cuts being much deeper and larger than others.

The pattern at G looks more elaborate than it really is. The size of the semi-circular shapes is decided by the gouge available. It need not necessarily cut the whole in one stab. In fact for this particular pattern it is better if it does not for a reason which will appear later. All one need do is to press in the gouge lightly and then slide it about halfway in its own cut and press down again so that the line of the curve is continued as in Fig. 13.

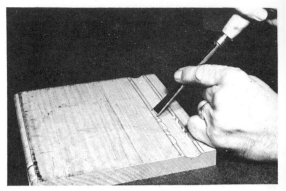

Fig. 11 First cuts in (I) Fig. 2.

Fig. 12 Removing waste, see (I) in Fig. 2.

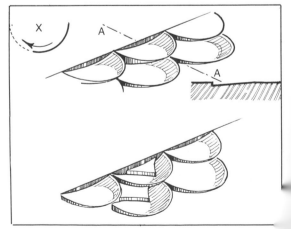

Fig. 13 *(top)* Fig. 14 *(bottom)* Stages in cutting (G) in Figs. 1 and 2.

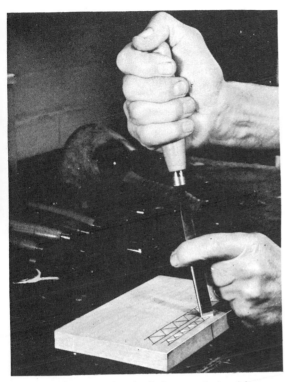

This is repeated until the semi-circle is completed. The waste is eased away with a narrow flat gouge as in Fig. 13, which shows the slope on the section line A-A. It is taken down as far as the surface of the small tongue or dart only. The shape of the latter is next cut in, and the cut at each side deepened (Fig. 14). It is here that the advantage of using the narrow gouge is realised. Again the wood is sloped away up to the dart. It is easier and more effective to use a fairly flat gouge for this rather than a chisel.

In patterns Fig. 2M and Q the wavy cut is made with a V tool, though if preferred a small veiner could be used. It is lightly sketched in first. Where small circular recesses have to be cut, as in O for instance, a small gouge of the required curvature is used. If this is lightly pressed down on the surface, partly revolved, and pressed down again, and the process repeated it will complete the circle, when it can be completely revolved with greater pressure. This will enable the core to be picked away with a small chisel. Sometimes it will come away with the gouge. The slight roughness left at the bottom of the recess is levelled by tapping down with a

Fig. 15 Downward stabs being made in chip carved detail. This is the first stage in forming the triangular pockets.

Fig. 16 *(below)* Removing the waste in chip carving. If possible the waste should be removed in a single cut.

punch filed to a flat end. A French nail of the required size can be used for the purpose.

Simple chip carving. This can be done with either chisels and gouges, or with one or two knives. The trade carver usually prefers the former, though chip carving does not often come his way. It consists of a series of pockets or recesses usually of reversed pyramidal form. The principle of cutting is the same in every case. Downward cuts are made first, the tool either upright or at a slight angle according to requirements, but so held that the cutting edge slopes, the corner reaching down to the deepest part of the cut, and the edge running out so that no cut is made beyond the shallow part.

An example is given in Fig. 15 in which a series of triangular pockets is being cut. A downward stab is made on each line, the chisel rocked forward so that its cutting edge is in line with the required slope of the pocket. Care must be taken to limit the cut to the width between the pencil lines. With the chisel held at a slight angle on its side the little pockets are cut as in Fig. 16. Each chip should come away cleanly without necessitating any scraping. The endeavour should be to complete the cut in a single movement, and with practice this can be done, though the direction of the grain needs to be watched, otherwise a split may develop in front of the edge and stray beyond the line.

Fig. 18 Preliminary downward stab in centre of pocket.

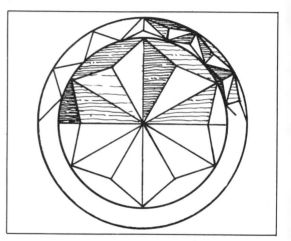

Fig. 19 Simple chip carving motif based on the circle.

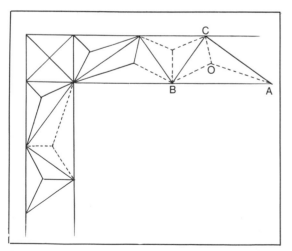

Fig. 17 Setting out chip carved border.

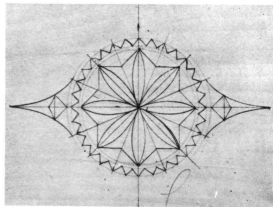

Fig. 20 Chip carving design set out on the wood

When the pockets are of reversed pyramidal form, that is, with the deepest part in the centre, it is necessary to cut in first on centre lines. These meet at a common centre and pass to the corners. In Fig. 17, for instance, the pockets are triangular, one being represented by ABC. Centre lines AO, BO, and CO are stabbed in first, the chisel edge sloping and with one corner on the centre O. Fig. 18 shows the idea. Each facet can then be sloped away in turn BOA, BOC, and COA. With practice these facets will all meet evenly on the centre lines. When the facets are curved it is necessary to use a gouge rather than the chisel.

Some care is needed in designing chip carving to avoid monotony. There are various ways of doing this, of which one is to limit its use to certain parts, leaving plain untouched areas. In Fig. 20, for example, the effect is much more telling than if the entire surface were covered with pockets. Another help is to start a main central shape—circle, square, triangle, or what you will—and make the rest of the pattern subservient to this. In Fig. 19 the circle is the main theme. Yet another way is to vary the size of the pockets. In Fig. 20, for instance, the circle of small pockets stands in contrast with the large centre pockets, and is far more effective than an all-over series of recesses of equal size.

Fig. 21 Figure in English Walnut, about 0.63m. (30in.) high. Carved by Juta Storch.

Chapter seven

Heraldic lion

This design makes excellent practice with the parting tool. In common with the leaf form given on page 36, it is intended as an exercise rather than a completed work in itself, and it is for the student to develop the ideas by making alternative designs.

The design is set out in squares for easy application, and transferred to the wood as already suggested (page 37). The material best suited to the design is oak, though the particular panel shown here is in mahogany.

Using the parting tool. Having transferred the design to the wood, the first move is to outline the design with a parting tool. Do not let the angle of the tool be too acute, say about 60 deg. Now steadily go round the design, cutting at a depth of approximately 3mm ($\frac{1}{8}$in.), no more; rather a little less if a choice has to be made. You will find that no difficulty is encountered if the tool is really sharp, except perhaps an occasional tearing up of the grain. This can be remedied by reversing the direction of the cut, and a clean outline will soon result. The design has a much more artistic and sculptural effect if the outline after cutting inclines slightly outwards rather than a definite right angle to the top surface. Undercutting never looks well in this form of carving.

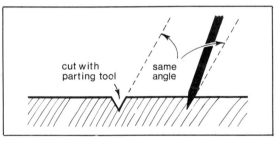

cut with parting tool   same angle

Fig. 2 Angle at which chisel is held when cutting in small detail.

Fig. 1 The design partly carved. A sharp parting tool is essential for work of this kind. Careful control is necessary in following the outline, but it makes excellent practice. Although the cuts are no deeper than 3mm. ($\frac{1}{8}$in.) the result is extremely effective. Modelling is little more than a sloping into the V cut outline, no attempt being made to round over the entire surface.

You will soon realise that the parting tool cannot be manipulated into the smaller parts of the design, and no attempt should be made to use it. Go as far as possible and then follow on with stab or set-down lines, made by chisels and gouges that fit the shapes. This can be done with the aid of the mallet · the palm of the hand. Keep the same oblique cut ade by the parting tool as in Fig. 2, then clear the

Fig. 3 The design set out in 25mm. (1in.) squares. There is no need to keep rigidly to this size. The squares could represent 22mm. ($\frac{7}{8}$in.) or 19mm. ($\frac{3}{4}$in.) if preferred.

waste wood away with, say, a 6mm. ($\frac{1}{4}$in.) flat chisel, linking up with the parting tool cut. The result should be a uniform cut outline throughout.

Modelling. Now to the modelling. First it must be remembered that the lion is purely decorative and is designed as such. Any modelling must therefore be done in a decorative way, rather than attempt to treat it naturalistically. Another point to remember in the modelling is that one must suggest the relief as a comparative basis; for example, two of the legs must give the impression of being in front of the other two, and the tail in the middle! To accomplish this you have only 3mm. to play with. Apply this rule to all other forms in the design and you will soon understand how essential it is to model only with very flat gouges, say 6mm. (¼in.) Nos. 3 and 4 and possibly No. 5.

Let all the cuts be considered first, then faintly draw them on the wood. Now cut freely with one of the gouges mentioned which you consider will give those subtle forms and shapes. Try not to merge these tool marks into the rest of the form. You will be tempted to do so. If it must be done with some cuts, then only the minimum.

Fig. 4 The completed design.

Chapter eight

Roundel

Figure one is a circular plaque or roundel with the edge turned to the section shown in Fig. 2. It could be cut out of 19mm. or 25mm. stuff. The structure of the design is geometrical as is obvious from Fig. 2, and is so arranged that the design could easily be adapted to any size of material you have by you. The carving illustrated was executed in oak, approximately 0·3m. in diameter. Walnut or mahogany would be good alternatives.

So far as the modelling is concerned this is a new approach, for, unlike the simple leaf form on page 36, there is little grounding necessary to produce the relief on the shape. Neither is there need to use the parting tool in the same deliberate way as when carving the lion.

The main shape or pattern is produced by fretcutting with a fine saw, and is an integral part of the design. For centuries pierced carvings have played n important part in decoration in Eastern and Jestern countries. I have particularly in mind the vely Byzantine capitals, the mediaeval screens in glish churches, and Georgian frames and pier sses, to mention but a few.

The planning of designs with piercings is not a simple task for each unit or shape must be linked up to another, producing shapes not only interesting in themselves but forming an important part in the whole design. To have small pieces unattached which at a slight touch would easily snap off (particularly *with* the grain) must be avoided.

Setting out. The method of setting out should be clear from Fig. 2. It is advisable to draw it first on paper before marking the actual wood. Over-all size might be 0·3m., and a circle of this diameter should be drawn in. A second circle, concentric with the first, is drawn in to mark the extent of the mouldings. Diameters at 90 deg. and 45 deg. are also needed, and should be drawn in with a set square.

The scroll shapes are based on small circles, and, since the narrow uncut surfaces interlace with each other, it is necessary to set the compasses so that the circles cut across each other and interlace to the extent of 3mm., the width of the uncut surface. When the position of one scroll has been fixed, the centres of the others can be also marked on the diameters equidistantly from the centre. A certain amount of trial and error marking may be necessary to obtain pleasing proportions.

The inner lines of the scrolls are also drawn in with compasses, and the volutes at the ends are based on circles struck from centres on these inner circles. It is clear from Fig. 2, however, that the ends of the scrolls and the volutes break away from the circle, and these parts have to be put in freehand. The leaf shapes between the scrolls are drawn freehand entirely. The small centre circle with its chip-carved pockets can be drawn with compasses entirely.

When all is satisfactory the whole thing should be drawn in afresh on the actual wood. Care in the geometrical setting out is essential to give a balanced result. For the leaves and volutes, draw one in carefully, and mark the others from a tracing made from it.

Carving the scrolls. The first essential is to pierce the openings, and by far the most satisfactory way is to have them fret cut by a good machinist. A ragged, uneven line is difficult to

Fig. 1 Attractive pierced and carved panel. Here the work is shown in stages. At the top the wood is marked out but is not pierced. The progress is shown working round clockwise.

Fig. 2 Setting out. All the fine lines are drawn in first with squares and compasses. Where the design diverges from these the lines are drawn in freehand.

correct. The alternative hand method is to use the bow saw, but this calls not only for careful following of the line, but necessitates the saw being held exactly square with the wood. It is inevitable that a certain amount of cleaning up with the file will have to follow.

Cutting the hollows of the scroll follows, and a straight gouge, say No. 8, 13mm. ($\frac{1}{2}$in.) is about right. The depth must be equal throughout, and a pencil line should be finger-gauged around from the front edge. In a hollow about 16mm. wide the depth might be 8mm. Where possible work *with* the grain, but it is inevitable that the tool will have to cut against the grain in parts. Work close up to the volutes, and then stab downwards around the last named, keeping the gouge about 1mm. from the line. Ease away the waste nearly down to depth, then cut in right up to the finished volute line.

In the disc in Fig. 1 the top and bottom scrolls are the easier to carve because the tool cuts *with* the grain as it approaches the volutes. The position is reversed in the two side scrolls, the tool cutting against the grain. The answer is to do as much of the work as possible *with* the grain and take fine finishing cuts at the ends. Really sharp tools are

essential, and it is helpful to make slicing cuts where practicable. Fig. 3 shows the carving in progress.

As seen to the left in Fig. 1, the volutes are slightly rounded over. This is not taken over the whole shape, but is rather in the form of a rounded chamfer around the edges.

Finally, the back of the carving is cut away around the piercing, with a bevel as in Fig. 4, which enhances the finish in front by giving a lighter appearance.

Fig. 3 Carving the hollow members.

Fig. 4 Back view showing chamfering.

Fig. 5 Decorative panel in limewood, about 46mm. (18in.) wide. Carved by Derrick Winwood.

Leafwork. The leaves themselves are left in projection with the groundwork sunk to the level of the quirk in the moulded edge. The simplest plan is to run around the outline with a V tool held to the waste side of the line. This can be seen in the top right-hand portion in Fig. 1. Note that it is continued right round the scrolls and into the volutes. This V cut will greatly help the following setting-in stage in that the gouge can be taken right up to the line without danger of being forced into the leaf by the wedge shape of the tool. The V cut relieves the pressure, enabling the wood to crumble away on the waste side.

The majority of the area can be taken out with a flat gouge, and finished off with a chisel. For the acute corners, however, a corner spoon bit or entering chisel can be used. The depth is only 2mm. full and can be judged by eye. Incidentally, when there is a lot of such recessing to be done it is a help to use a small router. Its purpose, however, is rather to test the depth than to actually cut the wood.

At the juncture of the leaves a small dart is formed. This is stabbed in at each side, and the wood sloped away with a narrow and flattish gouge.

Centre detail. This is chip carving in that it consists of a series of pockets which form radial leaf shapes in projection. The centre lines of the pocket are drawn and stabbed in with chisel and gouge as shown at the top in Fig. 1. The tool is held at an angle so that it cuts more deeply at the middle, running out to practically nothing at the ends. A gouge is used to slope away the waste up to these centre lines. Note that all facets meet at the same level. Small pockets are cut in the same way in the little triangular areas between the centre detail and the scrolls.

Chapter nine

Acanthus leafage

The probability is that the acanthus leaf has been more widely used in carving than any other motif. Invariably it is in conventional form as distinct from the naturalistic, and its form and treatment varies with the period and style. Sometimes it is highly stylised with square, spiky lobes as in Byzantine ornament, and in others it is used with elaborate scroll work so that it is difficult to tell where the natural ceases and the conventional begins. One feature, however, which seems to be common to all is that the leaf has pointed or rounded lobes, and is usually compound in that it is made of several smaller groups of lobes which join together and flow from one common vein. The groups nearer the stem tend to overlap those beyond, hence the typical arrangement of eyes and pipes at the juncture of the lobes. Fig. 2 shows the idea.

The emphasis given to these details, the degree of modelling, and the shape of the leaves varies with the style and period of the work.

The stages in working the leafage in Fig. 2, based on the Georgian style, are shown in Figs. 4 to 7.

Fig. 1. Acanthus ornament is perhaps the most masterly form of conventionalism ever introduced in decorative art. It was introduced by the Greeks and is based on the wild plant of the same name.

Legend has it, that whilst the marble blocks were lying on the ground ready for erection of a Greek temple, the acanthus grew up round it and the tips of the leaves turned over giving the impression of a volute, whilst the tendrils ran round the marble block like a carved moulding. This is well illustrated on this page.

Since then the ramifications have been enormous and made a great impact on practically all the artistic crafts. So from its introduction in Greece in about 400 B.C. to the Renaissance revival in England, it has influenced the enrichment of architectural forms and the artistic crafts in many materials.

Unlike the Tudor Rose or the Fleur-de-lis etc., the acanthus has no symbolic or national significance but by elimination in all that is accidental in art forms, it has become an abstract motif applicable to all crafts, serving artists and craftsmen alike in their quest for beauty of form.

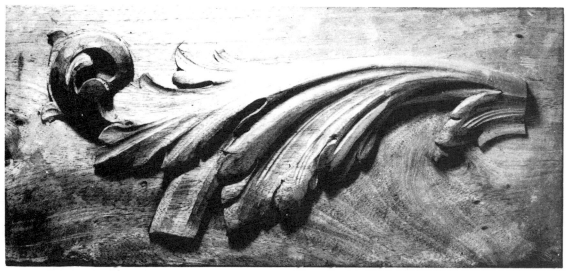

Fig. 2 *(above)* Bold and vigorous treatment in Grinling Gibbon's style

Fig. 3 *(below)* The design drawn out in 25mm. (1in.) squares.

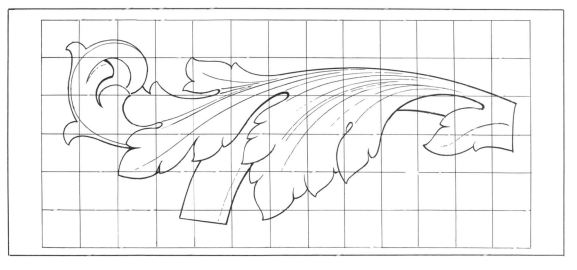

The form is quite bold with well-defined shapes and pronounced modelling. The panel, of any material, measures about 330mm. (13in.) by 150mm. (6in.) and is typical of the decoration that might have been used on panel headings, fitments, and general joinery in the first half of the eighteenth century. The wood is 25mm. (1in.) thick and the background is cut back to about ⸮mm.

The design. The design is first drawn out on paper (Fig. 3), care being taken to produce a natural flow to the leaves and to avoid a disjointed appearance. It is worth while spending time on this all-important work because no excellence of execution can compensate for poor drawing. When satisfactory, the design can be transferred to the wood with carbon paper. Preserve the original drawing because the marks on the wood are inevitably lost when the surface is modelled later, and it is useful to have the drawing as a guide.

Grounding. The recessing of the groundwork is the first operation, and this necessitates marking a line around the edges. It can be either gouged in or marked with pencil by the finger gauge method. Working from the edges inwards, use a fairly large half-round gouge such as a 19mm. ($\frac{3}{4}$in.) No. 9. The cuts can run out to the surface as the outline of the pattern is approached. It is easier to cut across the grain as it is less laborious and not so likely to splinter out the grain.

Fig. 4 Groundwork roughly recessed.

When roughed out in this way run around the pattern with a quick gouge or fluter (about 6mm. ($\frac{1}{4}$in.)), working approximately to the shape but omitting all detail, and keeping about 1mm. to 3mm. from the line as in Fig. 4. The idea is to make the cut on the waste side so that the outline can be set in with gouge and mallet, the wood crumbling away on the waste side.

Setting-in. With a fairly large flat gouge and using the mallet, cut in all round the main pattern, approximating the shape to the outline but omitting all small detail as in Fig. 4. Stop slightly short of the finished depth because the leafage has to be undercut later, and it looks bad to show tool stab marks on the groundwork. A fairly large flat gouge can now be used to make the groundwork flat down to the pencil or gauge line (Fig. 5).

Fig. 5 The leafwork bosted-in.

Modelling. Before any detail is put in the whole of the leafwork should be 'bosted' or 'roughed' in, making sure the highest parts, i.e. the top of the turnover and the main piping, are untouched at this stage. Also make a point of getting down to the lowest level, like the underneath of the turnover and the small spray of foliage nearby. Do not leave a little extra 'in case you spoil it'. This has already been provided for in the first stage of the ground-work yet to be cleared up. Remember you have given yourself a 13mm. relief carving to carry out, and you want to see the general effect in that relief before proceeding with details. In other words, make good use of the 13mm. In getting down to the lower part you will automatically 'bost-in' the intermediate modelling without concern of detail. This is an absorbing and interesting stage in all carving whether it be in relief or in the round, apart from increasing your confidence in free and

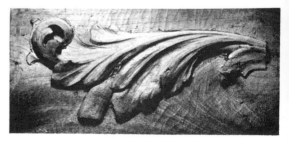

Fig. 6 Progress in the modelling.

Fig. 7 The outline set-in and undercut.

bold cutting. Cut in the 'eyes' of the leaf at this stage for it does establish permanent marks on which you can rely when redrawing the foliage on the wood, which a carver is continually doing whatever stage he is working on. The small fluter, about 3mm. ($\frac{1}{8}$in.) across the opening, does the eyes well. Gouges of various sweeps can be used for the modelling and a fluter for bringing up the pipings. Also, emphasising the main line leading to the turnover at the back gives an additional quality.

Good sweeping lines, with the tools mentioned, give a rhythm to the job which you should feel when cutting.

Do not try to make the surface dead smooth—tool marks give character to the work, though they must not be too coarse. Where the parts lie one over the other try to keep what would be a natural form. Thus the lobes at each side of the wide main stem should drop down to the groundwork as if by their own weight. Characteristic of this ornament is the rather blunt, rounded finish of some of the lobes which give added interest to the work. These are produced by using the inside of, say, a No. 3 or 4 gouge well bevelled on the inside.

At this stage the final outline and undercutting of the leaves can be completed, and the groundwork flatted to meet it. Finally a few deft cuts with a veiner along the direction of the leaves sharpens the whole and gives a sense of continuity and flow to the leaves. These cuts need to be made carefully but with confidence, and should be made in the required direction in a single continuous movement. If in doubt as to the final direction lightly pencil in the marks first. Figs. 6 and 7 show the further stages of the work towards its completion in Fig. 1.

Adam style leafage. A spray of leafage in different style is shown in stages of carving, pages 59 and 60. It is of the more delicate style used by Adam towards the end of the eighteenth century. The relief is comparatively slight, not more than about 6mm. ($\frac{1}{4}$in.), the ends of the lobes are rounded rather than pointed, and the general modelling is flatter. Fig. 8 gives the design set out in 25mm. squares, but the exact size is not important. Indeed, the design need not be copied blindly, providing the general feeling of the style retained.

Fig. 8 Adam style acanthus leafage set out in 25mm. (1in.) squares. The illustrations on page 60 show stages in carving the panel. In Fig. 9 the outline is roughly cut, and the background recessed. Fig. 10 shows the work partly bosted-in, and Fig. 11 a further stage with the final outline cut in. The finished panel is given in Fig. 12.

Fig. 9

Fig. 10

The design is drawn out on paper as in the previous example, and transferred to the wood in the same way. The groundwork is sunk back up to the general line of the design, no attempt being made to cut in the fine detail of the leaves at this stage (see Fig. 9).

Bosting-in follows as in Fig. 10, after which the exact outline of the lobes can be set in and slightly undercut as Fig. 11 shows. This will necessitate a certain amount of cleaning up of the groundwork — in fact this should be allowed for in the original setting-in, the tool being stopped slightly short of the finished level. Unless this is done there may be unsightly tool marks left on the surface.

Fig. 12 shows the last stage in which any final modelling is done and any cleaning up of the outline.

Fig. 11

Fig. 12

Chapter ten

Carved mouldings

No other section of the carver's craft has shown such a continuity of purpose as the decoration of mouldings. It is possible to establish a period in history by the style, shape, and cutting of a moulding. So, too, can we look back on centuries of work throughout Europe to give guidance when asked to enrich mouldings of today. The great difference now is an economic one, for, whereas there used to be no limit to the enrichment of mouldings in either quantity or quality, today we have to keep to a limited amount of well-placed ornamentation—which in many ways is all to the good.

As a matter of interest the following is one of many similar items from a 1697 account for work in St. Paul's Cathedral:

'For 2 upper Cimas of the great Cornice over ye Prebend's stalls, girth 4in. carved with leaves containing 186ft. run at 2s. 6d. p. foot £23.05.00.'

Today the approximate cost might £3—4 per foot.

Where today, however, carved mouldings have been introduced, as in many reconstructed public buildings, they do credit to the craftsmen who carved them. When mouldings are to be incorporated in the buildings it is the concern of the architect; or the industrial designer if he be concerned with the mass production of furniture; but in practice it is found that the craftsman, if he knows his job, is consulted at all stages in the design of the mouldings, with very satisfactory results.

Generally speaking, mouldings, like other aspects of carving in the trade, are divided into two—architectural and furniture, though they are not completely divorced from each other. In any case the method of setting out is applicable to both.

Furniture mouldings. From the nature of things furniture work is often stained and polished, and the small carved mouldings around table tops, cabinets, and chair work call for the polisher's attention. However, he has to deal with the job as a whole, and it is desirable to work on a surface, not necessarily very smooth, but rather with a crisp, clean finish. To achieve this, tools must be well chosen, preferably of the thin fish tail variety, with a shape that fits the outlines on both sides, well bevelled, and with keen edge.

Early English Gothic carving.

Architectural mouldings. Architectural mouldings such as cornices, architraves of doors, etc., of the Renaissance type, deep-cut or pierced mouldings of Gothic type, or flattish ones of the Jacobean period, require a different approach from furniture, both as to design and cutting. Each must be considered from its functional and siting point of view, in association with joinery work also, and very often gilding.

Working the moulding. When only a short piece of moulding is needed—a few inches—it is easy to work it with carving tools, but taken generally it is better to adopt the method of the joiner or cabinet maker. Today, mouldings in trade workshops are cut on the spindle moulder, four-cutter, or other similar machine. The man who has no such facilities must either use hand methods or use a portable electric router.

Use of the router. The electric router is shown in use in Fig. 1. It is a most effective machine for making small mouldings, but cannot tackle large sections—at least in one operation. It may be possible to work a large section with several passes of the machine, a different cutter being fitted to suit the section being worked. One disadvantage is that the range of cutters is necessarily limited, and they are expensive. Sometimes then it is necessary to design the moulding to suit the cutters available, not always a satisfactory arrangement.

The router is, however, invaluable for removing the bulk of wood down to the various square members, leaving the individual members to be worked by hand methods. Thus in Fig. 2 the required section is shown at Fig. 2A. The preliminary step is to cut the large rebate level with the small square member as at Fig. 2B. The carved members can then either be worked in their entirety by hand, or a series of cuts just short of the line can be made as at Fig. 2C, thus relieving the subsequent handwork. The circular saw can be used in the same way.

Hand methods. When only hand methods can be used the section can either be worked with moulding planes or with the scratch-stock. Planes produce clean mouldings and cut more quickly than the scratch-stock, but the disadvantage is that a wide range is needed to cover the many mouldings that may be required. Consequently most men use the scratch-stock with which an unlimited

Fig. 1 Routing a moulding along an edge using the fence.

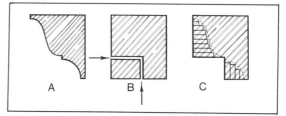

Fig. 2 Moulding and method of working. (**A**) shows the completed moulding, and (**B**) the preliminary cuts. At (**C**) the bulk of the waste is removed by a series of adjacent cuts.

range of sections can be cut since it is only necessary to file a cutter to a reverse of the required section.

Fig. 4 shows the tool. Two pieces of wood are screwed together and a notch cut in the two. The lower face of the notch is slightly rounded. The cutter, having been filed to a reverse of the section, is held between the two pieces by pressure from the screws. The cutter (which can be a piece of old saw blade or scraper) is filed straight across so that it cuts in both directions. Fig. 3 shows the tool in use. It is worked back and forth with the notch bearing against the edge of the wood, and removes the wood with a scraping action. It automatically ceases to cut when the full depth is reached.

Fig. 3 Working moulding using scratch-stock.

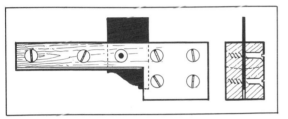

Fig. 4 Details of scratch-stock.

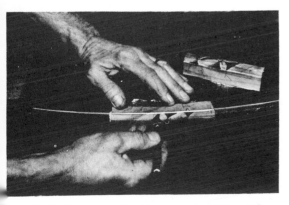

Fig. 5 Marking repeat pattern on moulding. It is generally more convenient and quicker to use a stencil brush. Thick water poster colour can be used

It is useless to attempt to work large mouldings in one operation with the scratch-stock. Anything much bigger than 25mm. (1in.) is difficult, and the only way is to take the individual sections independently. The man who is not used to it is advised to have the section machine-made at a mill. Incidentally, whatever the method used to work the section, never use glasspaper to finish off, because it is inevitable that granules of abrasive will become embedded in the grain, and these will rapidly take off the edge of the carving tools.

Setting-out. It is inevitable in carved mouldings that there will be repetition work, and their beauty is largely dependent upon it. Some means of rapid marking out is necessary. The most effective way is to make a stencil of one repeat and use this along the length, positioning it from the mark previously made. The stencil can be in thin pliable foil which will give to the section without springing back.

Generally it is convenient to bend the material closely into shape so that the position of the various members is obvious, then open it out flat to draw in the detail. It is not necessary to put in the entire pattern. Only the main features that indicate the repeat are required, the remainder being judged by eye and use of the right tools. If the shapes are then cut with the tools actually used in the subsequent carving, not only will the work be exact, but a great deal of time saved in picking up the right tools for the job. In the case of metal foil the edge of the tools will be slightly dulled in the cutting, but this is soon restored, and in the long run it is well worth it. Fig. 5 shows a stencil used for the repeat pattern around a table top.

Note that only main details are put in. Be careful to leave ties on the pattern so as to avoid movement of parts when stencilling on, and to avoid wanted parts dropping out. To mark the wood a water paint of the poster colour variety can be used, this being as dry and thick as possible to avoid overrunning beneath the edges. The brush should be a proper stencil brush, or any similar stubby brush used with a stippling movement.

Stages in carving. Now for the carving. The secret of successful carving of mouldings is to do the work in a series of definite clean cuts which can mostly be done in single or at most two cuts. It is not only quicker, but it gives the work a spontaneous, crisp character unobtainable in any other way. Anything in the nature of niggling or uncertain cuts or scraping kills this. The best plan is to try out one, or possibly two, repeats so that the system becomes clear and the range of tools obvious. The fewer the tools the better, and it is well to have only those required in front of you so that no time is lost in seeking for what is needed.

Simple leafwork pattern. In practice all corresponding cuts with one tool are made along the length of the moulding. In this way time is saved, and the repeats have a much better chance of uniformity. The sequence of operations of course is decided by the preliminary trial cuts. In Fig. 6, however, the stages of the work are shown side by side so that the method becomes clear.

First the small rounded depressions are cut in with a small half-round gouge. If this is started on the mark it can be revolved to complete the circle. Cut lightly with moderate pressure at first to make sure that the gouge follows the correct path, then press more heavily. It will be found that with slight side movement the little pip of wood will snap off and come away cleanly. As this cannot be controlled exactly, however, a small round punch is tapped in lightly with the hammer to make all uniform. The punch can be filed from a round nail of suitable size. Do not rely on the punch, however, for doing the work that the gouge should do, or it will give the impression that it was done by a machine.

The curved sides of the main leaf are now cut in, extending from the rounded depressions to the bottom. Stab a little deeper as the tool approaches the points of leaf and dart, bearing in mind that some wood has to be cleared away later. In a softwood hand pressure alone is enough, but in tough wood a tap with the mallet may be needed. Now slide the same gouge round to the lower part of the leaf opposite the dart, and cut in slightly deeper — down in fact to the groundwork. The hollow sides of the dart are next cut in, again to the groundwork, and the latter cut away with a flat gouge or chisel. This can generally be done in a single cut, unless the grain is very difficult. The chip should come away cleanly.

The dart has a centre ridge and slopes away at each side. This again can be cut with a single movement

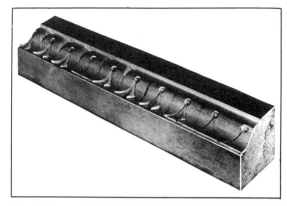

Fig. 6 Stages in carving conventional leaf pattern on an ogee moulding.

of a flat gouge. The experimental preliminary trial cuts show how deeply to cut, and the advantage of going along the length of the moulding making the same corresponding cuts becomes obvious. The knack of making them all alike is soon acquired.

Finally, the central incised cuts on the leaves are made with vertical stabs with a chisel. This runs out to nothing towards the tip of the leaf, and is formed by cutting vertically down, the corner of the chisel reaching right into the quirk, and then rocking the chisel over sideways until its edge reaches down to the limit of the cut. The wood at each side is sloped away into this central cut by using the gouge parallel with the moulding and raising the handle to form a curve (not a bevel) as the centre cut is reached. Using the gouge at right angles with the moulding and cutting in towards the back quirk is an alternative method. It may be necessary to clean up the depression at the quirk with a small skew chisel afterwards.

Another carved ogee moulding is shown in Fig. 7. The stages in carving can be read from right to left.

After stencilling, the wood at the front is removed down to ground work level in the same way as in Fig. 6. The slope on the darts follows, and finally cuts on the leaves. These are made with a downward stab followed by a single sloping cut, thus freeing the waste in two cuts only.

Astragal sections. Another section used considerably for carving is the astragal. On it carvers a all times have exercised their skill with wonderful results. On mediaeval screens, pulpits, etc. splendid carving was achieved, some sections being 100mm. (4in.) across, deeply cut, sometimes pierced, and often painted and gilded. They had a greater carving freedom, with the repeats not quite so mechanical as in the later Renaissance period. The heavy hollows and rounds of the Gothic demanded something bold in design and cutting, whereas the Elizabethans followed on with a flatter form both in section and treatment. Figs. 8 and 9 show this difference in style clearly. The following Renaissance period with its classical sections was not exactly an obvious continuation of English work of the 15th century, but rather something lifted from the Greek and Roman period during the revival of learning.

Coming of the Renaissance. It must have come as a great shock to craftsmen in Britain who, having worked for three centuries in the English tradition, were suddenly confronted with classical ideas and works of art, brought over by their patrons on returning from their journeys abroad.

Nevertheless a new style soon developed introducing the shallower, more refined types of moulding, the cymas, ovolo, scotia, torus, thumb, and the astragal. (See Fig. 10).

The astragal. We will confine our attention for a while to this, so far as carving is concerned. Fig. 11 shows the berry moulding at Fig. 11A, and B, the berry and sausage. In each case the setting out of the berries is essential. This can be done by pencil

Fig. 7 Alternative carved pattern on an ogee moulding.

Fig. 8 Pierced and carved gothic moulding. Note that the section is built up, the front portion being pierced, giving a wonderfully rich and dramatic effect.

Fig. 9 Carved Jacobean moulding. Compared with Fig. 9 the effect is much flatter, and there is not the same variety of treatment.

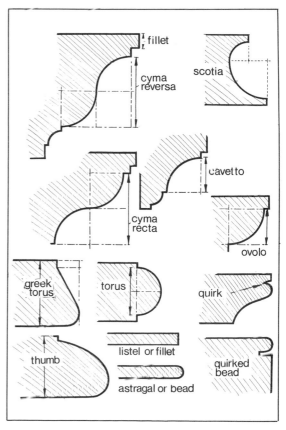

Fig. 10 Mouldings of the Renaissance period.

marks or better still with incision dots made by spring dividers to indicate the separation of the individual berries, as shown in Fig. 12. A chisel is then used to make a series of cuts across the grain as at Fig. 12C. The necessity for a very thin tool is obvious.

The gouge is started short of the chisel-cuts almost flat on the moulding as at Fig. 13A. It is then levered upwards and at the same time pressed downwards as in stages B and C. It thus cuts in the rounded shape, at the same time forming the semi-spherical shape of the bead. The tool best suited for the operation is a spade, well bevelled and sharpened well on the inside. The carver usually keeps one or two that just clip the astragal, which he calls his berry tools.

Many may find it convenient to thump the handle of the gouge lightly as it is levered over as better control is obtained. Be careful not to bevel the wood, for it is easy to make a pyramid shape. When the vertical position is reached a heavier thump is given so that the gouge cuts right down to the base of the berry.

Cleaning out the corners. The small waste corners between the berries are cut away with a small chisel, and they will generally snick away easily. Since most gouges are rather less than a semi-circle in section it follows that a part of the circle is left uncut. To complete the cut the gouge should be held upright and revolved with fair pressure. The trade carver of course realises this and can complete all gouge work before the corner chisel is used to lift away the waste corners. If the corners are not clean a small specially triangular-shaped punch that fits the diameter of the berry can be used lightly to finish them, but generally this is not necessary and is best avoided. Do not rely upon it to make the corners clean.

A word of warning is necessary here when a soft-wood such as pine is being carved. If the chisel is struck with the mallet to mark the initial separation of the berries it may easily snap the wood of the berries themselves, and this may not be realised until they are being shaped with the gouge. It is better to make a slicing cut across the grain with the chisel. In the same way it is generally advisable to cut each side of the individual berries first to avoid the same trouble.

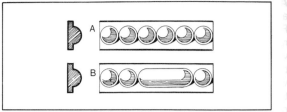

Fig. 11 The berry (A), and the berry and sausage (B) mouldings.

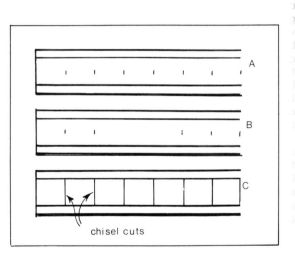

Fig. 12 Marking out the berry moulding: (A) Berry moulding spacing: (B) Berry and sausage spacing: (C) Preliminary cuts.

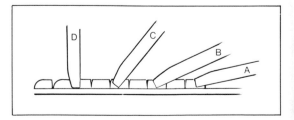

Fig. 13 Stages in carving the berry moulding.

Alternative pattern. An example of a small astragal moulding in stages of carving is shown in Fig. 14. Here a stencil would be prepared for marking out the repeat pattern. A series of downward stabs is then made on the main members and the wood sloped in at the side. In the case of softwood the downward stabs can be made by thumping with the palm of the hand, but hardwood generally needs a blow with a mallet.

Another and rather more elaborate leaf and ribbon moulding is in Fig. 15. Here the first cuts can be made with the parting tool where the ribbon is folded spiral-wise around the section. Next the centre berries are formed with a small half-round gouge, this being revolved round the diameter. The wood is then lightly sloped in at each side and the berry rounded by using the gouge hollow side downwards and levering the handle up as it follows the shape. In the case of softwood the outline of the leaves can be stabbed in straightaway, but if the wood is hard it may be necessary to set in directly on the line with the help of a mallet. Never take two bites at the outline if it can be avoided.

Sinking in the groundwork follows and this should follow the general rounded form of the moulding. Lastly, the turnover of the leaves is put in and the slight modelling cut with a veiner. Only a few shallow irregular cuts are needed to give the effect of the ribbon work.

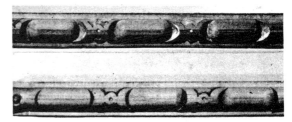

Fig. 14 Stages in cutting a carved astragal, right to left.

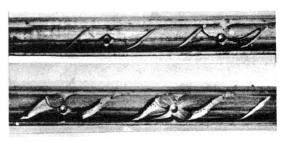

Fig. 15 Ribbon and leaf pattern in stages.

Fig. 16 Finely carved moulding of the Renaissance period.

A more elaborate acanthus leaf carving applied to a cyma recta moulding is given in Figs. 17 to 21. Here again a stencil template is needed. This can be in foil and is bent around the work as in Fig. 17. Fig. 18 shows the moulding after stencilling.

The preliminary stage of carving is to cut away the waste wood at the top, and here the groundwork is sunk back about 6mm. ($\frac{1}{4}$in.), care being taken not to lose the shape of the moulding. This is shown clearly to the left in Fig. 20, and in the dotted line in Fig. 22. The undercutting of the turned-over leaf in the main member follows (Fig. 20), and here again the section of the moulding should be followed. Finally, the leaves are modelled as shown in stages as in Figs. 20 and 21. A moulding of this kind calls for careful control of the tool in order to follow the outline of the various members.

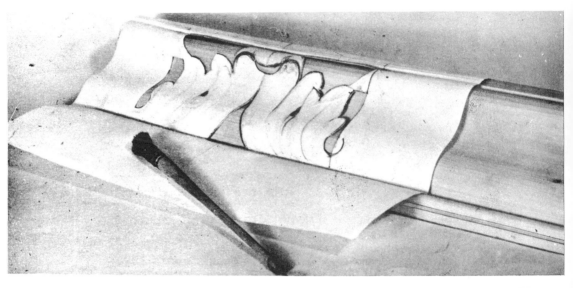

Fig. 17 *(top)* Preparing the stencil for the acanthus leafwork moulding shown finished in Fig. 21.

Fig. 18 *(below)* The moulding after stencilling. Only the main members of the pattern are cut out.

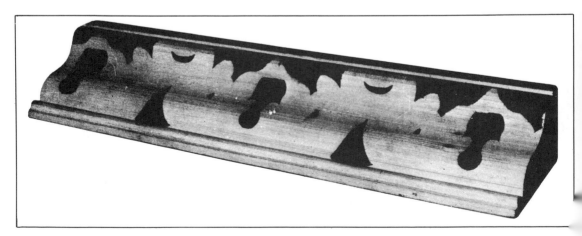

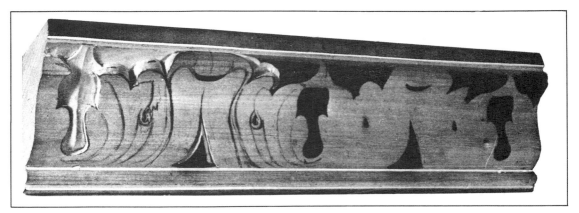

Fig. 19 First stage in carving. The background is cut back, following the general contour of the moulding.

Fig. 20 *(below)* Further stage in carving. The wood is cut away beneath the turn-over of the main leaf.

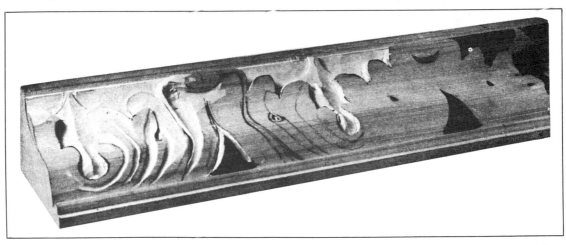

Fig. 21 *(below)* The completed carved moulding.

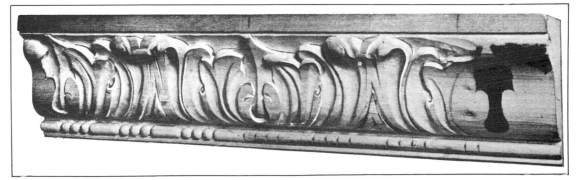

Mitres. A point not to be overlooked is the treatment of the mitres, both in the setting out and carving, whether they be mason mitres or the 45-degree panel mitres. Assume the former method of jointing is required on some oak panelling, with moulding stuck on the framing. The usual procedure is to run the section through on the rails, and stop them on the stiles to, say, about the width of material plus approximately 13mm. ($\frac{1}{2}$in.). The whole job is glued up and handed back to the carver who proceeds to continue cutting the moulding on the framework by hand to form mitre (see Fig. 23). Alternatively the moulding could be stopped on the uprights to form a square in which could be carved a patera as in Fig. 24.

Mouldings which are to be carved and mitred at 45 deg. are as a rule supplied by the joiner or cabinet-maker in random lengths, with the mitre lines in pencil clearly marked. If they are not so marked it is necessary to ascertain size of panels, and indicate on the moulding before any carving is attempted. This is vital to the spacing of the repeating pattern to be carved, and essential to the final fitting up and fixing.

In spacing out the pattern, as already suggested, allow approximately half a repeat on the inside of the moulding for the mitre. As with mason's mitre, the carver proceeds to finish up the mitre after the job is glued up. This equally applies if the mouldings are stuck on the solid framing. Try to keep clear of the actual joint when carving, for it can lead to little bits falling out. This can be avoided by giving the leafwork a centre stem as indicated in Fig. 25.

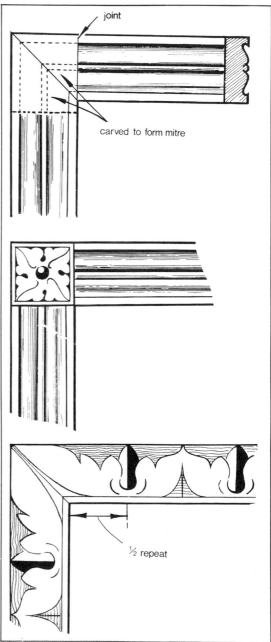

joint

carved to form mitre

½ repeat

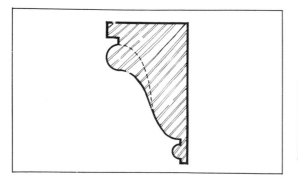

Fig. 22 Section required and how background is cut back (dotted line).

Fig. 23 *(top)* Carving mason's mitre.
Fig. 24 *(middle)* Patera covering corner.
Fig. 25 *(bottom)* Carving at mitred corner.

Chapter eleven

A task in which the carver and joiner are associated is the working of linenfold panels. Until the end of the 15th century English woodwork was not affected to any noticeable degree by foreign influence. Then came in Continental influence on some of the woodwork with its flamboyant tracery, carved shafts, and linenfold panels, like those at Carlisle cathedral and the church at Charlton-on-Otmoor. The linen panels at Carlisle are extremely simple in character, the top of the moulded panel being finished off as a section of the panel itself by setting down the outlines and grounding out the background sufficiently for housing into the framework (Fig. 2).

Linenfold panel

Early linenfolds. This form of panelling, emerging as it were from nearly three centuries of Gothic tradition, started something new. It developed rapidly, and like so many forms of motifs which began in a simple way, lost a good deal of its beauty and purpose when craftsmen took the lead with plane and later the spindle, and left design to look after itself. The result today is, in many cases, panelling of heavily cut hollows and rounds, bearing no resemblance to folds whatever. Those in Fig. 3 are a fine development of the early ones. They are in slight relief, and the finish at the ends gives a quality which is difficult to improve upon, particularly when they alternate in a run of panelling.

The remarks appertaining to simplicity in design, and the rather shallow relief of the early examples, should be borne in mind when trying out original designs. Remember, too, it is a conventional form of linen which you wish to interpret in wood which either a joiner or carver could undertake with tools available without complicated sections. You should look around churches, museums, and other public buildings to widen your scope in design. There are particularly nice ones on the late mediaeval pulpit shown In Fig. 4 where the moulded folds are cut into the panels, the highest members being flush with the front face of the panel itself. The bottom is nicely shaped, and the top of each panel has tracery work planted on.

Some of the early sixteenth-century examples have foliage springing from the centre moulding, and some Flemish ones of the same period have foliated sides and ends. These, like many others, tend to become carved wood panels rather than linenfold.

Fig. 1 Panelling in oak carved with linen ornament from a fifteenth century farmhouse (now destroyed).

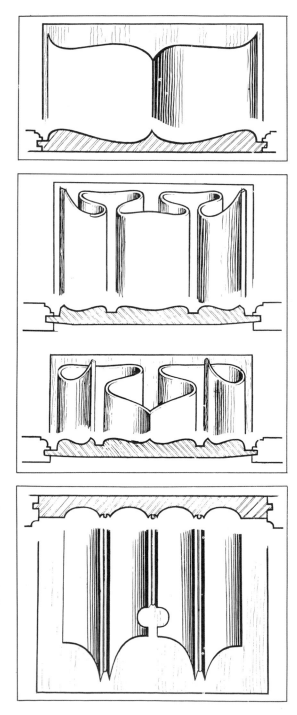

The panel in Fig. 5 is founded upon a series of panels in a fifteenth century pulpit in Westminster Abbey. The depth of the undulations is about 13mm. ($\frac{1}{2}$in.), and the wood therefore needs to be 19mm. ($\frac{3}{4}$in.) or 22mm. ($\frac{7}{8}$in.) thick.

The design. Draw in the design on paper, and put in an end view showing the folds as they actually lie one over the other. This is important because without it it is impossible to draw a section to which the wood has to be worked. The reason for this is that, whereas the undulations of the panel represent the front folds, they bear no relation to the back folds. The end view (see Fig. 6E) shows the actual folds, enabling the section D to be put in. This in its turn shows the positions of the preliminary grooves to be made in the panel C.

The last-named cuts can either be made on the circular saw or with the portable machine router. Alternatively, those who have no access to a machine can use the hand plough. Note the varying depth to which the grooves are taken.

Working the undulations. The purpose of the preliminary cuts, of course, is to help in working the undulations. They form a positive guide when using the moulding plane. First, however, a rebate should be worked around the four sides, this being taken down as far as the groundwork. The idea is given in Fig. 7 which also shows the preliminary cuts along the length.

For the hollow parts of the folds, round moulding planes are used, and at least two are needed. The only awkward section is that marked X Fig. 6 as it is not easy to reach down to the acute corner. The writer's plan is to run a tenon saw down the corner first, and use the small round plane as far as it will reach. The hollow is finished with a knife shaped like the blade of a penknife, used with a scraping movement. The side-rebate plane is also handy.

Rounded parts can be formed with the rebate plane, set coarse for removing the bulk of the work, and fine for finishing off. A large round file is handy

Fig. 2 *(top left)* Simple pattern from Carlisle.
Fig. 3 *(middle left)* Two patterns in low relief.
Fig. 4 *(bottom left)* Panel from a late mediaeval pulpit.

Fig. 5 Based on 15th century panel at Westminster Abbey. The left-hand part is completed, and that to the right in process of being carved. Note that this is the true linenfold, in which the folds can be followed in their entirety across the width.

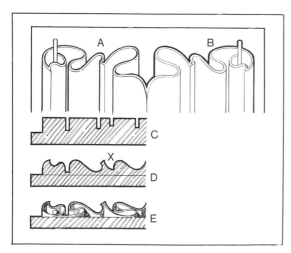

Fig. 6 Setting out of panel in Fig. 5: A Shape to be carved: B Line to which background is cut away (heavy line): C Preliminary grooves: D Section to be worked: E End view showing folds.

Fig. 7 Panel with preliminary grooves worked.

Fig. 8 Undulating section completed.

for reducing the facets of the hollows. To finish off use coarse glasspaper wrapped around shaped wood rubbers until the facets are smoothed into continuous curves, and finish off with a fine grade. Fig. 8 shows the panel after moulding.

Marking end shapes. The first stage in the actual carving is to free the pattern of the unwanted wood down to the level of the groundwork, and this involves drawing in the outline of the folds on the undulating surface. It is a little awkward, but it is only a matter of measuring down from the end at various points and fairing in curves. Having completed one side a piece of tracing paper can be pressed into the shape and the lines marked. The same paper can then be reversed into the opposite folds.

Although the outline of some of the folds will automatically disappear as the carving proceeds, it is advisable to put it all in. For immediate purposes, however, the outline up to which to cut the groundwork is required, and this is the thick line shown at Fig. 6B. Cut down on the line, but stop a trifle short of the groundwork. The reason for this is that the folds have to be slightly undercut to give a realistic appearance, and if the cuts are too deep at this stage they will show later as blemishes. It is a

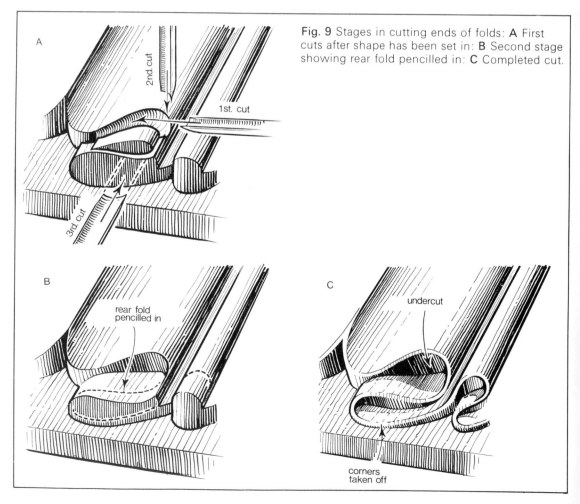

Fig. 9 Stages in cutting ends of folds: **A** First cuts after shape has been set in: **B** Second stage showing rear fold pencilled in: **C** Completed cut.

A

2nd. cut

1st. cut

3rd. cut

B

rear fold pencilled in

C

undercut

corners taken off

help to go around the outline first with a small, quick gouge worked on the waste side. Then when the shape is set in, the wood crumbles away easily.

Cutting the end shapes. Fig. 9 shows the stages in cutting the shaping of the folds. At Fig. 9A a cut is made with a fairly quick gouge to the waste side of the outline, working across the grain. The undulations of the intermediate and rear folds must be kept in mind, remembering that they must appear to be one over the other. Second and third cuts remove the waste giving the effect at Fig. 9B. This is also shown to the right in the unfinished portion in Fig. 5. The outline will have to be pencilled in afresh where chips have been removed to mark the folds afresh.

The undercutting follows as at Fig. 9C. This is confined to the edges which are more or less horizontal. At the sides of the folds the gouge will have to be taken in practically horizontally (the panel lying flat on the bench), and a point that becomes at once obvious is that an appreciable thickness of wood must be left because the wood would crumble if reduced to paper thickness. It is for this reason that a double line is drawn in on the original drawing Fig. 6A.

Finally the extreme edge of the folds can be taken off at an angle to show a slight thickness Fig. 9C. The extent of this varies in different panels. In some it is almost non-existent; in others it is a full 2mm. wide. A keen narrow chisel is the best tool to use for this, following round the curve, keeping the width equal throughout and making the slope to the front constant.

Fig. 10 Linenfold panel from an old house. Although there are over 200 panels in the room each is slightly different in detail from the next.

Chapter twelve

Trays with pie-crust edgings

A delightful detail of the eighteenth century was that known as the pie-crust edging, used widely on small table tops. Its chief use was on the circular tops of small tripod tables, the centre portion being recessed. In the best work the whole thing was cut in the solid, the edging being cut with carving tools. Clearly, however, this involved a great deal of work, and a cheaper method sometimes followed was to use a thinner top, make the moulded edge separately, and plant it on. Apart from taking much less time it tended to give a cleaner finish. In the hands of a good carver, however, the solid carved method gave excellent results, and was more satisfactory in that there was no failure of glued joints to fear. The tray in Fig. 1 has its edging carved in the solid.

The circular form of tray is the simplest to carve, at any rate for those with a lathe, because the whole of the centre part can be recessed by turning. This leaves only the edge to be fretted and carved by hand. If the tray is elliptical or rectangular the centre portion can be removed with the portable machine router. If only a hand router is available a series of 'walls', should be left against which the face of the router can bear, these being afterwards chiselled away. The whole thing is finished later by scraping.

Tripod table with piecrust edging and bird cage movement.

Fig. 1 Detail which is also suitable for a table top. The main recessing of the centre part is done on the lathe, but the moulded edge is carved in its entirety.

To be able to lower almost the whole of the centre recess on the lathe is clearly much quicker than carving or routing away. It is for this reason that the circular form of top is favoured for the pie-crust edging. All of the forms in Fig. 10 need carving or routing or a combination of both.

Setting out. The setting out for the tray in Fig. 1 is given in Fig. 2. This is 0·3m. diameter. If slightly larger a similar design could be followed, but if a much bigger tray or top is needed it is necessary to include an extra repeat of the pattern, or possibly two. Decide on the number of repeats, and divide up the circle into the same number. In Fig. 1 there are four repeats, hence the arrangement in Fig. 2.

The small hollows can be drawn with compasses, these being centred on a line just outside the main edge. The centre part of the serpentine shape can also be struck with compasses, but the ends will have to be put in free hand. Draw one complete repeat of the shape on paper so as to be sure of a satisfactory spacing, and cut a template of one half of the repeat in card, giving the inner as well as the outer line of the moulding.

A little reflection shows that, although most of the centre recessed portion can be turned, only a limited part of the moulding can be done on the lathe. It is worth while doing even this limited amount, however, because it is a check on the section and helps to ensure uniformity. Fig. 3 shows part of the edging, and the finished section is given at Fig. 3A It is clear, however, that it can be turned to the extent of Fig. 3B only. The hollow represents the true section at the curve at its inner-most point. The same thing applies to the inner edge of the top bead. Any attempt to take these outwards further would cut away wood beyond the line. In the same way the top outer corner is rounded to form the bead, but it cannot be taken in farther.

Turning. Cut the wood full to an approximate circle and centre it on the face plate with a piece of waste wood of about 19mm. (¾in.) thickness inter-posed. It can be fixed with screws as the holes are covered over later by baize to be glued to the underside. Turn away the centre up to the inner limit of the edging (Fig. 3) using scraping tools. It should be perfectly flat but no glasspaper should be used as this would tend later to take the edge

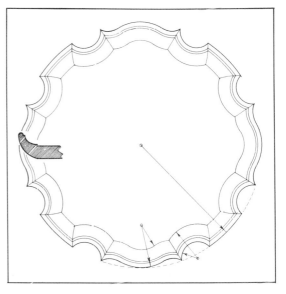

Fig. 2 Setting out of shape and section through edge.

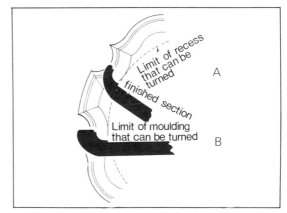

Fig. 3 Sections showing finished shape and extent to which edge can be turned.

from the carving tools. The edge itself can be turned to the section at Fig. 3B again no glass-paper being used. Fig. 4 shows the work at this stage.

Cutting the shape. Remove from the face plate, and divide the periphery into the number of repeat patterns. Using the card template already prepared, mark the outer edge with pencil. The waste can be sawn away on the bandsaw or jigsaw (if available), or it can be cut by hand with the coping saw. Clean up the shapes using a half-round file, making sure that all corresponding shapes are alike. The file is taken straight across square.

Carving the moulding. With pencil draw the bead parallel with the outer shape, using the finger as a gauge. This is given in Fig. 5, which shows how the waste wood is cut away as far as the bead down to the depth of the fillet or square. The simplest way is to first go round the line with a small veiner held on the waste side. Then when cutting down with gouges which approximate to the curve the waste wood crumbles away easily. Finally, remove the waste with a flat gouge down to the level of the fillet.

The inner and outer lines of the hollow have now to be marked, and this is awkward owing to the undulating surface. Fig. 8 shows how it can be done with a scratch-stock having a notch cut in it to hold a pencil. Round the bearing shoulder of the stock so that it will engage the curves, and run

Fig. 5 Edge fretted and bead partly carved.

Fig. 4 Disc turned to shape showing moulded edge.

Fig. 6 Extent of hollow marked and waste removed.

Fig. 7 Carving completed showing moulding parallel all round.

finishing off and to ensure a flat surface. It is as well to go over the entire centre as this will take out turning marks and remove any slight undulations.

The carving of the hollow member follows, and is probably the most difficult part because of the wide variation in grain direction. Remove the bulk of the waste with a fairly quick gouge, following the grain as far as possible. With a flat gouge which approximates to the line of the mitres (note that some of the mitres are slightly curved) cut down each mitre vertically to a depth *slightly* below the finished surface (see Fig. 11). This gives a definite line up to which to work when carving the hollow.

In some cases the gouge works *with* the grain when cutting into the mitre and cutting is simple. In others it has to cut against or across the grain, and matters can be helped by part revolving the handle so that it cuts with a slicing movement.

The bead will also have to be carved along its entire length, and a similar method will have to be followed. Razor sharp tools are essential for a clean finish. With a gouge in really good condition

Fig. 8 Inner edge of moulding being marked. This enables the pencil to pass over the undulations of the hollow member.

round the entire edge allowing the pencil and stock to lift up or down to suit the undulations, and keeping the tool radial to the curve.

This gives the marking in Fig. 6, which also shows the flat centre surface cut away up to the edging. Note the grain carefully when doing this, working *with* it as far as possible. The scraper is useful for

Fig. 9 View of back with rounded bevel partly carved.

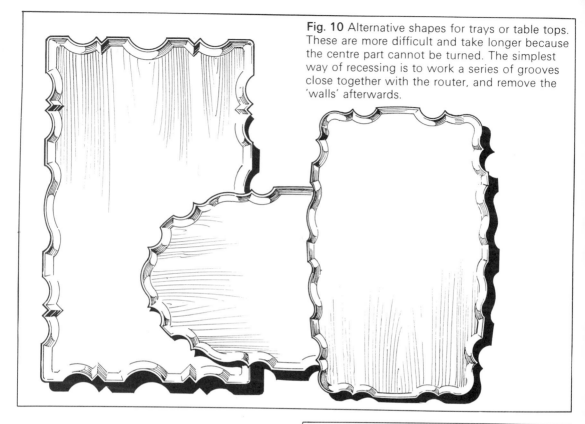

Fig. 10 Alternative shapes for trays or table tops. These are more difficult and take longer because the centre part cannot be turned. The simplest way of recessing is to work a series of grooves close together with the router, and remove the 'walls' afterwards.

it is possible to work even against the grain providing thin cuts are made and the tool is used with a slicing action.

Back. The back of the tray is carved so that the same shape is continued all round. The extent of the shaping can be gouged round with the scratch-stock by the method shown in Fig. 8. A view of the tray from the back is given in Fig. 9.

Finishing. It is extremely difficult to give a result which can be french polished or varnished using carving tools only. Most workers finish off with glasspaper because the edging is really only a moulding. A shaped rubber is handy for some parts, but the glasspaper held over the finger is effective. Begin with *Fine* 2, followed by No. 1 or *flour*. A flat block is needed for the centre, and a specially pointed one is handy to reach into the corners. Hold it flat and work *with* the grain.

cut down with gouge

Fig. 11 Preliminary mitre cut. Note that some of the mitres are slightly curved.

For a mahogany tray bichromate of potash gives an excellent colour. This can be followed with french polish or plastic lacquer. The latter is the simpler to use owing to the many awkward inner corners. Apply with a brush, giving, say, four coats well rubbed down between each. Flat down with *flour* paper lubricated with soap, and finish off with an abrasive motorcar polish.

Chapter thirteen

Gothic carving

Scrolled leafwork (Fig. 1). The design can be drawn out on paper in full size, taking the details from Fig. 2. There is no need to keep exactly to the design—in fact it is all to the good if the reader attempts his own variation on the basic theme. Make the foliage well fill the spandrils with good shapes so characteristic of this form of conventional leafwork. The sections in Fig. 2 show the shape to which the parts are modelled.

Recessing the groundwork. This is taken down about 6mm. or 8mm. and, as the wood is oak, it would be risky to attempt to set in with gouge and mallet as it would probably result in a gashed or fractured edge to the tool. It is far safer to go around the outline with the parting tool, holding this to the waste side of the line. When later the shape is set in the wood crumbles away on the waste side. It is not possible to follow all the small intricacies of the design, but this does not matter. It is only the main sweep that need be cut.

Whilst the parting tool is being used, a cut can be made at each side of the centre raised part of each lobe. This marks their positions and gives a start too in the later modelling process. Fig. 3 shows the work at this stage. The section at Fig. 3B shows the V cuts clearly. Note that the cuts defining the rounded centre of the lobes are shallower than those at the edges.

When working at an angle across the grain it will be found that one side of the V tool is liable to tear out the grain whilst the other leaves it clean. It is therefore necessary to consider which is the best direction in which to work it. One side of the cut is important; the other does not matter. Work in the direction which gives a clean finish to the side that matters. Take, for instance, the portion of Fig. 3A. It is clear that the tool should be worked in the direction shown by the arrow because the left-hand side of the V will give a clean finish to the stem. The right-hand side which is liable to tear out is only part of the background which has to be cut away.

Incidentally, the keener the cutting edge the less liable it is to tear out—in fact, a really keen carving

Fig. 1 Scrolled leafwork

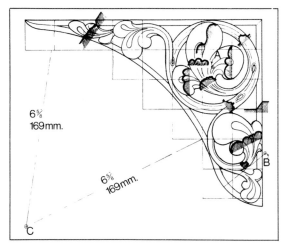

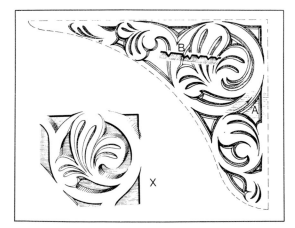

Fig. 2 Design set out in 25mm. (1in.) squares.

Fig. 3 First stage, showing outlining with parting tool. At X the groundwork is sunk and the leaves ready for modelling.

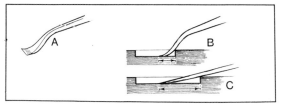

Fig. 4 How grounding tool can be used in small recesses.

tool can often be taken against the grain without tearing out, providing that only thin chips are removed. There are occasions on which the only way the tool can be used is against the grain, and this is when a razor-like edge is essential.

Sinking the Groundwork. Now follows the setting-in and recessing of the groundwork. Selecting gouges which fit the shape, work all round the outline of the lobes and scrolls, stopping, however, at places where the first named overlap the scrolls. Hold the tools so that an upright cut is made. It is not likely that the tool will be taken down to the finished depth in one cut; it is invariably necessary to remove some of the groundwork and then cut down again. In any case, stop short of the finished depth because the work is bound to need correction and cleaning up later, and it would not do to leave unsightly tool marks.

A certain amount of waste can be removed with an ordinary straight gouge, but to finish cleanly a bent chisel or grounding tool is invaluable (see Fig. 4). This can be used in recesses of much smaller size as shown at Figs. 4B and C. For the wider spaces a No. 25, 6mm. ($\frac{1}{4}$in.) size is suitable, and a 3mm. ($\frac{1}{8}$in.) for smaller ones. You will also need a 3mm. ($\frac{1}{8}$in.) corner grounding tool for getting closely into acute corners. This is similar to the tool shown at Fig. 4A but the edge is sharpened askew. Fig. **3X** shows the appearance of the work when the background has been recessed. Note that the outline which encloses the carved area finishes with a bevel. Consequently, the setting-in should be done around the inner line, the bevel being cut afterwards.

Modelling. In the modelling which follows observe the sections in Fig. 2 and work *with* the grain as far as possible. It may mean that a cut will have to be started in one direction and finished in the other owing to the changing direction. On this score note that it is a tremendous advantage to be able to work with either hand. It saves having to release the wood and turn it round. Endeavour to work in long, deliberate cuts and avoid little niggling chips. You won't attain perfection straightaway, but it is a technique for which to strive. This is particularly the case when modelling the scrolls in which the facets should run in long, unbroken sweeps.

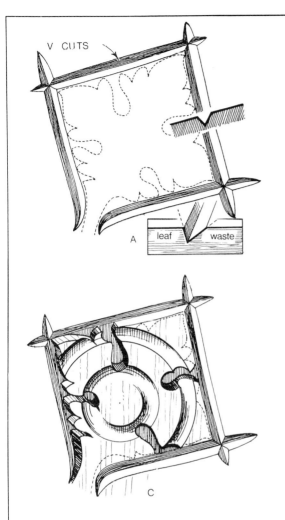

V CUTS

leaf   waste

A

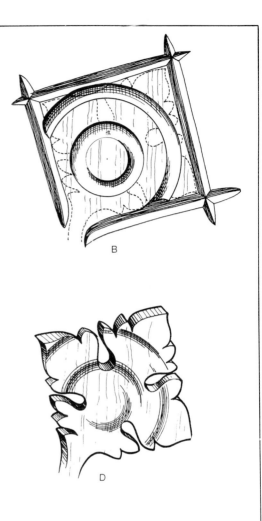

B

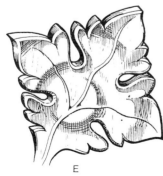

C

D

Fig. 5 Modelling of the leaves of corner shown in Fig. 6

E

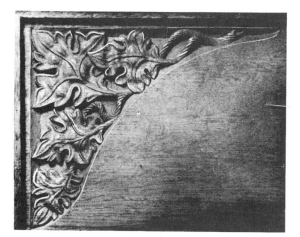

Fig. 6

necessary. It will be seen from Fig. 6 that the leaves undulate, and if this were done after final setting-in it would result in the outline crumbling. The method shown in Fig. 5 is therefore followed. Straight cuts are made with the parting tool to define the approximately square form of the leaf as at Fig. 5A. This gives the general form. Two circular cuts are now made with a small No. 9 or 10 gouge as at Fig. 5B, these giving the positions of the main undulations. The setting-in can then be completed, Fig. 5C, or the edges of the hollows can be rounded over as at Fig. 5D. Finally the veins can be outlined with a small veiner or parting tool, and the wood at each side smoothed as at Fig. 5E. This diagram also shows how a bevel is run around the outline of the leaves.

For a start you can round over the scrolls, using the No. 5, 6mm. ($\frac{1}{4}$in.) gouge with the hollow side downwards, and put in the hollows afterwards with the No. 5, 3mm. ($\frac{1}{8}$in.) gouge. For the small eyes where the scrolls branch from each other, make a downward stab with the small veiner, No. 11, 2mm. ($\frac{1}{16}$in.), and cut the long sides with the Nos. 5 and 4, 6mm. ($\frac{1}{4}$in.) gouges. The narrow grounding tool will remove the waste chip.

The ends of the raised portions of the lobes are cut vertically with a gouge which fits the shape. Then, by holding the tool low down with the hollow side downwards the rounded shape can be given. Start about 3mm. or so back from the downward cut, and as the tool moves forward raise the handle so that the horizontal cut changes to an upright one. For the long sides use gouges which fit the shape and work in long strokes with the hollow side downwards. Be careful to avoid digging in the corners.

Note that immediately in front of the raised centre the lobe is hollowed. This can be put in with the 6mm. ($\frac{1}{4}$in.) No. 8 gouge and the edges sloped away with flatter gouges.

Variation A (Fig. 6). With one exception the general procedure of marking out, setting-in, and recessing the groundwork is much the same as in the previous example, Fig. 1. It is mainly in the general modelling that a special treatment is

Crown copyright.

Fig. 7 Screen in oak. Dutch, 1692.

Fig. 8 *(right)* Monkey carved in the round in oak. Carved by William Wheeler.

Chapter fourteen

Gilt electric lamp

The lamp in Fig. 1 was made for general table use rather than as a reading lamp. Thus it is of good height, 0·48m., and throws its light over an entire dining table. In general style it follows the Italian Renaissance, and is oil gilt, though it would look still more attractive if parts were water gilt and burnished. Thus certain members of the mouldings and parts of the scrolling could be finished in this way.

Construction. It consists of five main parts; the top sconce, the dish beneath it, the main column, the surbase, and the base. The latter in its turn is made up of a centre piece to which the wood for the three scrolled feet is fixed. Fig. 2 shows the lamp in part section, revealing how the parts fit together. At the top of the main column is a dowel which passes through the dish into the sconce. A similar arrangement is followed at the bottom, a dowel going through the surbase into the base. Note that the three feet of the base are held to the centre block with two 9mm. ($\frac{3}{8}$in.) dowels each.

If the design is set out in full size the exact plan shape of the base can be ascertained; also the thickness of the parts needed to hold up the shape. This is shown in Fig. 2. It is advisable to complete all construction work first, including the turning of the upper parts, before proceeding with any carving. Remember in the turning to allow enough wood for the leafage to be carved. Thus the turn-over of the leafage of the main bulbous part of the column needs the rounded contour shown in the part section, and the whole of the lower part is about 2mm. fuller than the top so that the leaves appear to be wrapped around a plain baluster. In the same way sufficient fullness must be allowed in the base for the scrolled leafage to be carved.

All parts are cut out and jointed but are not glued together until carving is completed. The base, however, is regarded as one unit, the three radiating pieces for the feet being glued on. They have to be cramped, and it is a help to leave the outer edges square without any shaping as it is otherwise awkward to apply the cramps. As the parts join at 120 deg. it is advisable to glue on one only at a time, otherwise the cramps may be in the way of each other.

Fig. 1 *(left)* Gilt electric table lamp. Height is 0.48m. (19in.).

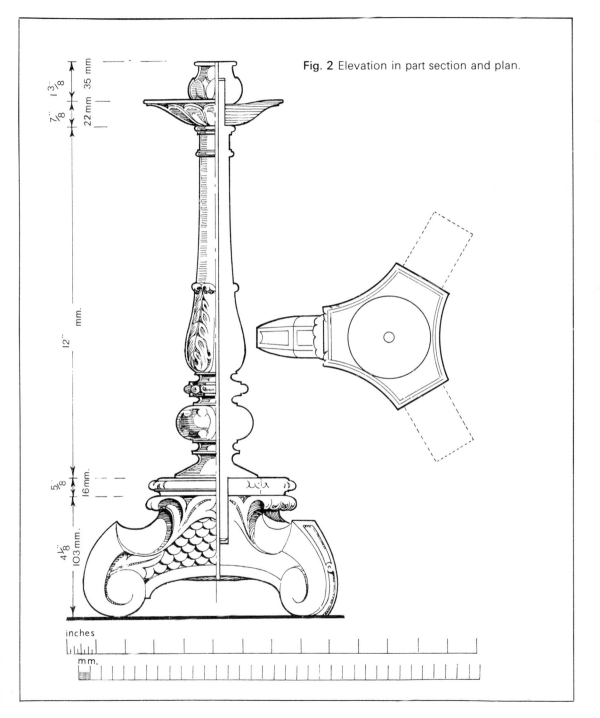

Fig. 2 Elevation in part section and plan.

35 mm
1 3/8"
7/8"
22 mm

12"   mm.

5/8"
16 mm.

4 1/8"
103 mm.

inches

mm.

Having assembled the base the **three main** surfaces can be hollowed out to a sweeping curve. Much of the waste can be removed with a flat gouge, and the sweep finished with spokeshave or a large flat-shaped half-round file. When all the three are satisfactory and uniform the outer shaping can be sawn and finished with spokeshave and file.

Another method often followed in the trade is to turn the entire base, the contour being that of the outer shape of the scrolls. The cut-away portions are then sawn away on the bandsaw. The advantage is that all outlines correspond exactly, and individual jointing of the feet is avoided. On the other hand it is usually necessary to laminate as it is difficult to obtain so thick a piece of wood to hold up the shape, and many small lathes have not sufficient clearance to enable the work to swing. It is usually a matter of considering the job in accordance with circumstances.

Carving the column. There are four leaves around the bulbous part, and the easiest way of spacing is to step round with dividers by trial and error until there are four equal spaces. As the leaves have central veins each space is divided into two. At each mark draw an upright line, holding the stem vertically in front of the eyes, as it is thus far easier to judge the truth of the lines.

The lobes of the leaves are best spaced out by the one-third system. The over-all height is divided into three, and the tip of the lowest lobe placed at the lower mark as at Fig. 3A. The remaining distance above is again divided into three and the second lobe taken at the lower division Fig. 3B. The process is repeated at Fig. 3C until as many lobes as are required are marked.

The first step in the carving is to cut in the series of triangular pockets formed at the adjacent lobes (Fig. 4). Set in with a narrow gouge which fits the shape, and lift away the waste with a bent corner chisel. As it is difficult to finish cleanly it is convenient to finish off with a specially made triangular punch filed from a large french nail (Fig. 5). The end is filed flat and the rounded sides filed to triangular section. Do not attempt to use it in place of the gouge. Its purpose is solely that of making the bottom of the pocket flat.

This forms the main outline of the leaves, and the limited modelling follows. The main vein is put in

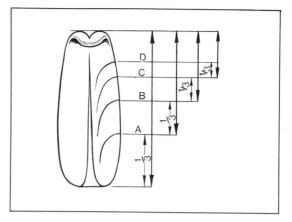

Fig. 3 Setting out of acanthus leaf.

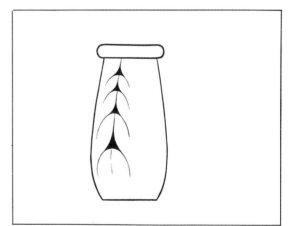

Fig. 4 Diagram of leafwork.

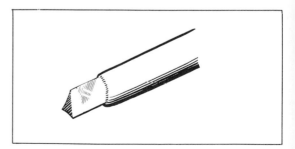

Fig. 5 Punch for levelling triangular pockets.

with the V tool, and the wood sloped into it at each side with a flat gouge. The effect of the lobes folding over each other is produced by stabbing downward with a gouge and easing away the wood at the side. At the juncture of each bottom leaf with the next is an eye which can be formed with a small veiner. Complete by cutting the turnover of the leaves at the top. Note that the centre of each tip (which of course is the back of the leaf) has a V-shaped depression which is actually the end of the main raised vein in reverse.

To form the sausage and berry detail in the lower member use a gouge which is of the same section as the member or a trifle larger. The method of cutting is dealt with on page 66.

Only shallow cutting is needed on the bottom ball member. Pencil in the shape, and set in around the outline, using gouges to fit the shape. Carve in the wood to form the scrolls, leaving the latter untouched. Note also that the centre of the area between the scrolls is untouched and retains the original shape. Lastly, cut a flat hollow on the straps, lightly rounding over the circular terminals.

Surbase. The plan shape of this is roughly an irregular hexagon. The long sides curve in to follow the hollow plan shape of the main base, and the edge is worked to a beaded or astragal section. Simple leaf detail is carved at the points, and the main bead section is tucked in locally below the leaf. The actual moulding itself can either be carved by hand or can be worked on a machine router or spindle. The hole for the dowel of the column should be bored from each side.

Base. This being assembled and the plan and elevation shapes worked, the line of the scrolls and main leafage should be put in. Note how the wide band of the scroll widens progressively as it leaves the volute. The centre part with the scale ornament is recessed to a depth of a full 2mm., and the scale ornament is formed by stabbing down with a gouge of suitable curvature, and sloping the wood into it with a fairly flat gouge (see also detail at Fig. 13, page 44). Cut in the deep hollow on the top of the scroll. Note that this is opposite in section to the lower part in that it is hollow rather than rounded. At the edge where the leaves from each side meet, the leaf form is continued across. It is rather awkward to finish the deep recess beneath the turn-over of the leaf tips, and a bent

Fig. 6 Early carving stage. The parts are not glued together until carving is complete.

tool is useful. Along the outer edges of the scrolls a shallow recessed panel is cut. Use a narrow gouge to outline the shape and a nearly flat tool to level the groundwork between. It is seen clearly in Figs. 1 and 7.

The bottom surface of the base is shaped with gouges to a curve. Any other tools such as spoke-shave and scraper can be used to finish off to a smooth surface.

Dish. This is turned, and has a hole right through it to enable the top dowel of the column to pass through. The top surface is hollowed. Note that when being turned a square fillet is formed below the rounded edge. This is a great help in that the tips of the leaves align with it, ensuring regularity. Cut in the divisions between the petals with the parting tool, and make the rounded tips spring from them. These round tips are cut in with a gouge of suitable curvature, and the waste eased away.

Sconce. Here the turning can help the carving in that the tips of the leaves can line up with a member formed in the turning. The eight main petals are stepped round with dividers, and separated with the parting tool at the base. The top shape is drawn in freehand and the line cut in again with the parting tool. This enables the waste to be removed down the level of the underlying leaves. The latter are cut in lastly. The sides of the veins are outlined with a narrow veiner. The cuts are fairly deep at the bottom and run out to nothing at the top. The wood at each side is curved into them, leaving the edges of the petals untouched.

Assembly can be in a single operation. Cramping is not essential, but if cramps are used they should be tightened over two pieces of wood. This will enable them to clear the dish and base. Use a square piece of wood at the bottom, the size of which just clears the base; at the top a plain piece of the same length as the square is used. Thus the cramps are both upright and parallel when applied. Only light pressure is needed.

Gilding follows, and can be either oil or water; or a combination of both. Certain of the highlights would look specially well if water gilt and burnished. Instructions on the two processes are given in the relevant chapters.

Fig. 7 Carving nearly completed.

Chapter fifteen

Polished and gilt elliptical frame

This attractive frame is carried out in mahogany and is polished on its main flat surfaces. The carved detail of the frame itself is oil gilt, and the cresting water gilt. If preferred the whole thing could be gilt, but the contrast between the polished wood and the gold is particularly pleasing.

Frame construction. This could be made in various ways. That shown in Fig. 1 is made in four pieces fixed together with halved joints as shown by the solid and dotted lines in Fig. 2. In another way it could be in two pieces dowelled together. In this case care would have to be taken to place the dowels so that they do not emerge at the surface when the wood is moulded and carved.

Whatever method is used, the whole thing should be drawn out in full size on paper. The best shape is produced by the pin and string method given in Fig. 3. Only the over-all outer and inner lines need be drawn in, but a section through the frame is advisable as in Fig. 2. The lines of the halvings are put in with a straight-edge as shown.

From this drawing a template of one of the pieces is made of cardboard, the shape being traced through. This enables the parts to be marked out economically on the wood, the shapes being one within the other in any convenient way. They are best cut out on the bandsaw, but failing this the bow saw will have to be used. Cut the halvings, and glue up, assembling on the drawing so that the correct shape is maintained. Make sure that it is free from winding.

As all subsequent moulding and rebating will have to be done from the inner shape, this latter should be carefully cleaned up with the spokeshave, making sure that a fair, unbroken line is formed, and that the edge is square. Easily the most satisfactory way of working the section is to use either the spindle moulder or the router. If neither is available the only way is to use the scratch-stock, but in this case it would be more satisfactory to plant on the main outer moulding. Otherwise a great deal of waste would have to be removed, and it would be an awkward job at best.

Fig. 1 *(left)* Elliptical mirror in mahogany with gilt detail and cresting. Size over elliptical frame is 0.61m. (24in.) by 0.47m. (18½in.).

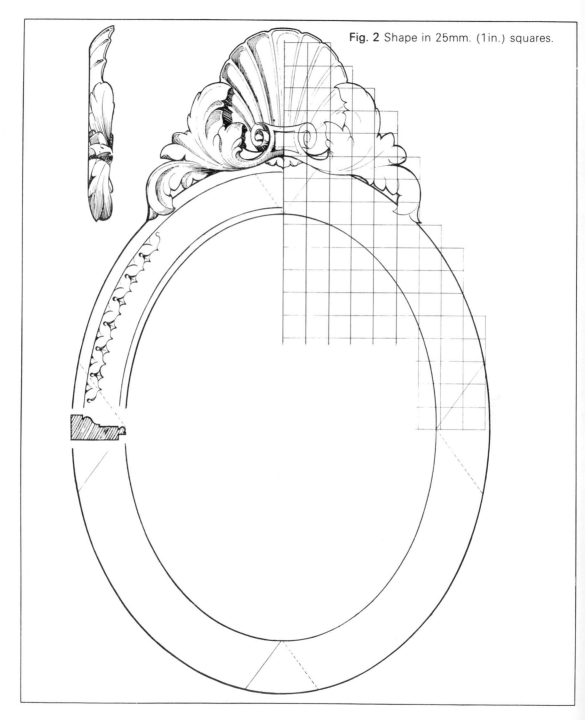

Fig. 2 Shape in 25mm. (1in.) squares.

Fig. 4 shows the section being worked on the machine router, the latter being reversed and bolted beneath a table. Fig. 5 shows the stages in working on the router. Incidentally, since both spindle and router machines rotate in one plane, it will be necessary to work the rebate quirks at Fig. 5F by hand, using the scratch-stock.

Carving the frame. The repeat leafwork pattern should be tried out on a spare piece of wood, because it is desirable to make the pattern to suit the gouges available, and to use as few tools as possible. In the frame shown the entire outline of the leaf was cut with a single gouge 9mm. ($\frac{3}{8}$in.) No. 8 and the waste removed with a small chisel. The eyes were cut in with a 3mm. ($\frac{1}{8}$in.) No. 9, and the curved stem with a 9mm. ($\frac{3}{8}$in.) No. 7. The sharp edges were taken off with the small chisel, making four tools in all.

There is no need to set out the whole thing fully. It is enough to mark the centres and ends of each repeat as a guide for placing the gouge. Working from the sample, step round the pattern with dividers. When, say, half-a-dozen repeats from the starting place, try out to see whether the spacing is true. If not increase or decrease the setting for these last few repeats. Any slight difference will not show.

Start off by sinking the eyes, holding the gouge at an angle and turning the handle round in a circle so that a flat rounded depression is formed. Any unevenness or raggedness is afterwards corrected by tapping each eye in turn with a rounded punch made from a french nail filed to the required shape.

Fig. 6 shows the stages in carving the pattern. Cut boldly on the line straightaway and clean away the waste with a single cut, or at the most two. Repeat patterns of this kind rely for their effect upon clean unhesitating cuts. The notes on carving the moulding on page 64 should be read, as the carving is practically the same, though the cutting is rather more awkward owing to the ever-changing grain direction around the curve.

Sausage and berry. For the sausage and berry carving a small spade tool should be used, one which just fits the berry shape. The method of cutting is given on page 66. As the grain in parts is specially tricky, it is a great help to cut in the divisions between the berries with a superfine saw.

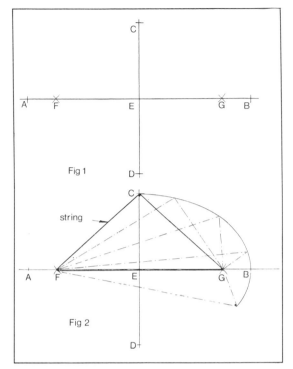

Fig. 3 Setting out ellipse by pin and string method. Draw axes AB and CD intersecting at E. With radius AE and centre D mark AB at F and G. Drive pins at F, G, and D, and tie fine stretched string around as shown by heavy line in lower diagram. Withdraw pin at D and substitute a sharp pencil. Keeping string taut move pencil so describing the ellipse as shown.

Fig. 4 Working moulding and rebate on router.

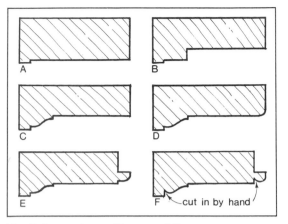

Fig. 5 Stages in working moulding.

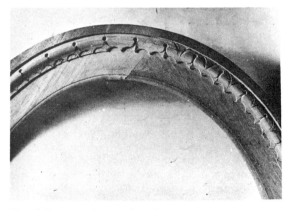

Fig. 6 Progress in carving frame.

Fig. 7 The frame marked out and partly carved.

In the ordinary way a thin chisel can be used, but owing to the constantly changing grain direction some of the detail is inclined to snap off. This does not happen when the saw is used.

To form the berries the spade gouge is held in the centre of the berry, the handle nearly horizontal. In a combined movement it is pressed forward and downward, the handle being gradually raised until it is vertical. It is taken first in one direction, then in the other, the semi-spherical shape thus being formed by a combination of the shape of the tool and its movement. This is explained more fully on page 66.

Cresting. Stages in carving this are given in Fig. 8. Select a pleasant carving wood such as lime, plain mahogany, agba, or yellow pine (do not use parana pine). Draw out the elevation in full size, and transfer to the wood. Fret out the outline, and cut to fit over the top of the oval frame.

Begin by cutting back the shell, leaving the leafage passing over it. For a start it is only necessary to keep approximately to the line, leaving the final setting in of the leaf shapes until later. When bosting-in the leaves remember that they are not merely flat shapes, but undulate considerably. The main top leaf, for instance, should be rounded in section, so that its side elevation appears as the side of the leaf, not a mere thickness. This is shown in Fig. 2, side view.

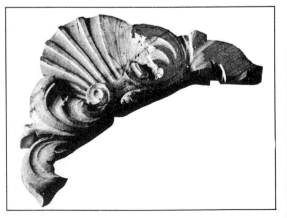

Fig. 8 Cresting with carving more advanced.

The thickness of the wood is about 28mm. (1in.), and full advantage should be taken of this, the shell curving backwards from the top to about 6mm. ($\frac{1}{4}$in.) thick to immediately above the scrolls. In the same way the lobes of the leaves should be at different levels within the thickness. Work the tool in the direction of the veins, forming sweeps free from kinks, whether viewed from front or side.

The flat surface of the frame and its edge should be french polished, leaving the carved work to be gilt. Details of gilding are given in Chapter 20.

Fig. 9 *(below)* Fine quality frame carved in mahogany. An 18th century piece of the highest quality. It was cut from a block 119mm. (4$\frac{3}{4}$in.) deep, the carving being three-dimensional. The design shows great imaginative quality, and the execution is superb. 0.57m. (22$\frac{1}{2}$in.) high by 0.44m. (17$\frac{3}{8}$in.) wide.
Photo: Victoria and Albert Museum, London. Crown copyright.

Chapter sixteen

Lettering

Carving incised lettering, an interesting yet exacting task.

We all know that lettering in any way presented is symbolism. Its purpose is to convey a message quickly, expressively, and in the crafts, beautifully. Also it should be in a form associated with the subject, and in a material which will enhance it. In a parallel sense this is achieved in heraldry and many forms of ecclesiastical symbolism. Each is distinct in itself by virtue of the particular materials used, yet in general giving the same message. The lion of England may be expressed practically by the printed word; it may also be the lion rampant in an heraldic achievement. So also could it be the lion of St. Mark on an embroidered banner or carving. The difference is in the artist's ability to put over in fine drawing a good design with a high standard of technique in a material of which he is the master.

General considerations. This is important to remember if you are to achieve the best in lettering. It is true that there is a tendency for some craftsmen to have the design and spacing set out by someone else, which he in turn accepts and carves. This is one method but it is not the best. At its highest, lettering, whatever the style and size, or the material, should be the product of one artist-craftsman.

This chapter on lettering deals for the most part with the technique of the subject, but it must be stressed that well-cut letters in themselves are not enough. They must be beautiful in shape, whether in isolation or in word arrangement; and when in composition and spacing they must still retain that beauty.

The general layout of carved wood inscriptions must be free from any type-looking arrangement, that is, in the printing sense; nor must it give the impression that some mechanical device was used in the setting out. Each job must be considered as an individual work, from a point of view of siting its relationship with any architectural work surrounding it, the lighting it will receive when completed, whether in relief or incised, and the treatment it may demand in colour, or gilt, or both.

Setting out. The setting out and spacing of lettering in the first place is one of the most difficult things to write about, or instruct in, for no two works present the same problems. If rules are given to help, they can be broken immediately by the very nature of the next work. For instance, I can suggest that the space separating two words is the size of, say, the letter O, or the line separation is two-thirds of the height of the letters, and other generalisations, but it never works in practice. In some cases, as in massed inscriptions, the letters and spaces have to be compressed, and in other instances it is necessary to elongate the lines. It becomes obvious, then, that there are no golden rules or quick methods which one can lay down for the successful spacing of carved lettering. These are gained solely by experience and knowledge, plus a good understanding of tools and the materials to be employed on a particular job.

Pencil lay-outs. Now for a little practice. Draw on paper the shape full-size in which your lettering is to be spaced, and round it draw smaller shapes (say 50—75mm.) but in the same proportions as the full-size one. On these try out thumb-nail sketches in various arrangements to include all the lettering required, without the aid of lines or other guides as in Fig. 1. Make any words which you wish to emphasise appear important. Include both massed arrangements and symmetrical ones, and try all the possibilities of composition you can by the different arrangements of words and spacing. You will find this work interesting, and suddenly amongst your many scribbles you will find some arrangement that appeals to you.

Now from your selected small sketch transfer your idea to the full-size panel nearby. For this you will require T and set squares to enable you to interpret full-size your little selected sketch. Draw lightly with a soft pencil the whole of the inscription with the aid of a good example of lettering, say that from a Trajan column.

Before leaving this drawing make sure it is a well-spaced, carefully lettered composition, for on this will depend the success of your panel.

Fig. 1 Preliminary small sketches for lettered panel. The small rectangles are to be the same proportion as the full-size panel, and several arrangements should be sketched in. The selected one is then copied into the full-size panel.

Fig. 2 *(right)* Alphabet cut in Roman capitals. This panel is 0.38m. (15in.) by 0.26m. (10½in.) and the letters 44mm. (1¾in.) high.

Hints on setting out. From my experience in designing and cutting letters the following should be of use. Roman capitals are better suited for carving than lower case, though the latter may be used with equal success. If the inscription is to be of larger letters, say two inches or more, readability is improved by larger spaces between words and lines than, say, letters of approximately one inch. Try to prevent lanes of empty spaces that appear to run through the whole layout. Sometimes it is useful to count the number of letters to be carved and roughly divide them up to suit the number of lines which you consider will make up a nicely proportioned panel, adding one letter for each space between words. It never works out exactly but is certainly a guide. Incidentally, you will not get any good results with incised letters under 13mm. (½in.).

Never mix up different styles of lettering on the same panel, though larger letters of the same style can be used to emphasise particular words. If the panel of lettering is to be framed in the joinery sense the framing or a moulding around it must be considered in the final layout. The smaller the letters, say 19mm. to 31mm. (1in.), the more they may be grouped or massed together, and by the nature of things will be read more easily; whereas larger letters up to 150mm. (6in.) appear more in isolation as far as legibility is concerned. For this reason extra precision may be given to accuracy in drawing and cutting.

You will gather from the remarks above that all lettering is relative. My observations regarding the planning and layout of lettering that has to be carved is not applicable to the individual letters and their shapes. Good shapes can be accomplished as from the outset you can be guided by fine examples. Well-drawn alphabets are easy to come by today, in books and portfolios; also photographs of cut examples. Do not take too seriously, however, the point of view of some given on the anatomy of each letter, particularly when set squares, compasses, and protractors, etc. have to be brought into action to produce one letter. If the artist-craftsman of today had to do this he would weary of their talk, and, like those of yesterday, would never produce those grand examples of which we are so righly proud.

Of course you must draw the alphabet over and over again from good examples. Then with the

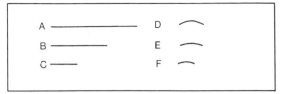

Fig. 3 Shapes of tools used in carving the panel in Fig. 2.

Fig. 4 Early stage in carving the panel shown completed in Fig. 13. The letters at the bottom are practice cuts.

shapes perfected you can create words and sentences with a rhythm and assurance which is practically instinctive. Bear in mind that the ultimate result, plus spacing and composition, will alone be the criterion of good lettering. A good exercise for beginners is to obtain a good sheet of Roman capitals about 25mm. (1in.) in height, or use those in Fig. 2, which were cut in oak. On tracing paper and using a pencil carefully trace by hand, then destroy. Do this daily until such time as you feel competent to produce the same letters without reference to the originals. By doing this daily as an exercise, you will at least have the basis of good letters.

Marking out. Here I assume that you have a well-designed panel of lettering on paper, and a panel of oak trimmed to size. Make sure that it is not figured, for this can be very irritating and confusing when cutting incised letters. Make a point, too, of having the grain horizontal, as cutting across the grain gives crisper and sharper work. There are times when this is not possible, in which case a parting tool would help considerably if the grain runs in the other direction, more so in the case of the larger letters, above 37mm. (1½in.). In cutting *with* the grain and using flat chisels there is a tendency for the grain to splinter beyond the serifs, with results which cannot always be remedied. The use of the parting tool does help to prevent this.

The lettering now has to be put on the wood, and the usual practice is to trace on the wood from the original drawing using carbon paper. I find this a cumbersome method, for in the process the tracing might slip a little, and, however slight, this can be disturbing. Another point is that the carbon paper always makes unwanted marks, and to get rid of them often calls for the use of a scraper, which in turn might ruin the lettering already carved. Furthermore, the panel may have been specially prepared as far as finish is concerned.

By far the better method, though requiring more skill, is to rule the lines embracing the letters with a T square and soft, sharp-pointed pencil. Now with the original drawing in front of you mark free-hand, word by word, the thick or upright arms of each letter, checking up as you go. If necessary use dividers to see you are not overstepping the size of words as allotted in your drawing. Likewise indicate the other letters in a similar way, not bothering in any case with serifs, etc. The tools will produce these without drawing.

I find this a cleaner and quicker way, and little has to be done at the finish of the cutting except to clean up the odd pencil marks with indiarubber. Practice that way from the outset, for it will en-

courage confidence and give better results. This method is always followed successfully by sign writers.

Letter cutting. Now for the actual cutting. For your guidance, the number of tools used for cutting the incised alphabet, Fig. 2, was six, and the shapes are as indicated in Fig. 3. All are carving chisels and gouges, spade shape, though firmer chisels can be used for all the straight members of the letters. After some practice and experiments you will find the spade shapes are easier to handle. They give a clearer vision when cutting.

Generally speaking, the straight members of all letters are best stabbed at the centre, using chisels approximately 6mm. (¼in.) short of their length. Thus 25mm. (1in.) letters need a 19mm. (¾in.) chisel which cuts just short of the serifs; 31mm. (1¼in.) letters need a 25mm. (1in.) chisel; and so

Fig. 5 Cutting in centre line of letters. If possible use a chisel which completes the length in one cut. It avoids all irregular joining marks.

on. With really large letters, say about 50mm. (2in.) and above, the parting tool can be brought into operation with good results, providing you do not try cutting the serifs with it. It needs more skill but is well worth trying. In the panel illustrated in Figs. 4 and 13 lines were drawn across the panel to help the spacing and cutting the serifs, but after some practice this can be dispensed with, for the linking up of the straight-cut incision with the serifs will come almost automatically as you speed up. Although a vertical centre cut for each letter is necessary, there is no need to draw it in because it is quite easy to judge the midway line between the two outer lines.

The panel is cramped down over a solid part of the bench, and a cut made along the centre line of each letter with chisel and mallet. If the wood is hard, such as oak, do not attempt to go down to the full depth straightway—unless the letters are small and therefore not deep. Rather, chop in moderately and then slope away the wood at each side, stopping well short of the outer lines. Final cuts can then be made right up to the lines. The advantage of the wide chisel will be obvious since all joining up of narrow chisel cuts is avoided. Often these final cuts can be made with hand pressure only, or possibly with a thump of the open hand, but for really hard wood the mallet may be needed.

The angle is in the region of 55 deg. A lower angle than this produces a rather flat result in which the shadows which give form to the letters are largely lost. On the other hand, a higher angle means that more wood has to be removed without any gain, and that the ends, particularly the serifs, are awkward to cut.

To enable the chips to come away cleanly the sloping facets must meet on the centre cut, but avoid making the latter over-deep. An open cut at the bottom of the letters looks unsightly.

At this stage it is better to do all the vertical centre line chopping and the preliminary sloping cuts first—or at any rate line by line. The reason is that the final sloping cuts call for a really keen edge, and, as the chopping down dulls the edge rapidly, it is better to get all this part of the work done first, and sharpen the chisel afresh to enable all the fine finishing cuts to be made.

There is no point in making the centre cuts on the whole panel first because the position of the panel would probably have to be shifted on the bench, but it is certainly an advantage for one or possibly two lines. For the shorter straight parts, such as the horizontals of E, for instance, a narrower chisel will have to be used. Fig. 5 shows the centre cuts being made, and Fig. 6 the sloping cuts.

Curved members. The curved sections of some letters are at first awkward to deal with and it is a case of selecting gouges which best suit the particular curve in the central stabbing and cutting. In some cases it may be necessary to use two or possibly three gouges to complete one curve. Make sure they are the right sweep. Improvisation can lead to all kinds of mistakes in the process of cutting. Where difficulty is found in shaping up the curves with the gouges selected, try using a flattish

Fig. 6 Cutting in the sloping sides. The cuts from each direction must meet exactly on the centre downward cut.

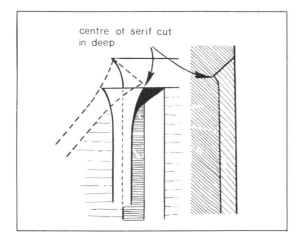

Fig. 7 Cutting serifs. Note increased depth.

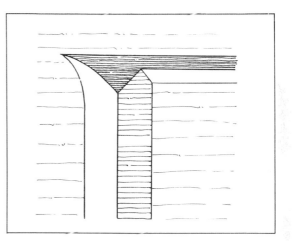

Fig. 10 How wide and narrow incisions intersect.

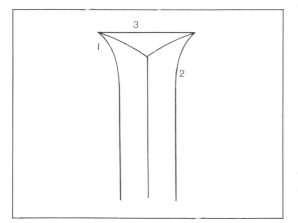

Fig. 8 Order of cutting serifs.

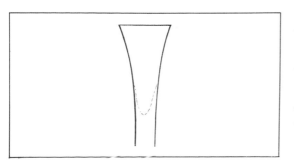

Fig. 9 Spade chisel for serifs.

gouge (which has been suggested for the serifs) and with a slicing movement follow round the entire curve, in the direction which best suits the grain of the two sloping facets of the curves. The outer is the easier to cut. Those parts running in the direction of the grain call for special care.

Serifs. Having cut the straight and curved parts, the serifs have now to be dealt with, and it is well to complete these line by line, as in the case of the other incisions. One tool only is necessary, and from experience it is found that a 6mm. ($\frac{1}{4}$in.) spade gouge with a sweep of, say, a No. 3 tool is ideal.

Fig. 7 shows the first stage. The tool is held on the sloping side of the letter and is pressed forward and twisted sideways and slightly downwards at the same time. This side movement enables the gouge to reach into the curve of the serif and link up. Thus the straight part of the letter is continued into the curved serif in an unbroken line. This leaves just the end to be sloped in, and enables the waste to be lifted away cleanly. Fig. 8 shows the stages. For larger letters, however, it is advisable to cut down the centre lines of the pocket first (much as in chip carving) and slope away the sides and top of the pocket into them. In all cases of incised letters the centre depression of the serifs—that is where it joins the main stem—is cut deeper than the rest of the work. It gives better results that way.

The form of the serif where a narrow horizontal member meets a wide vertical one calls for consideration, because the wide one is necessarily deeper than the narrow one. The treatment is shown in Fig. 10, in which it will be seen that the narrow (and consequently shallow) member runs out into one sloping side of the wide one only. This is a detail which scarcely shows in small letters, but must be followed when large letters are cut.

A point in connection with lettering in which there are several lines, is that it is always advisable to finish off one line *completely* before starting the next. It often happens that a small detail is left, the carver saying to himself that he will return and correct all such imperfections afterwards. The truth is, however, that they are invariably forgotten or overlooked, and it is therefore better to make sure that every line is in order as it is finished.

Cleaning up. When the entire panel has been carved there will necessarily be some pencil lines left in and these have to be cleaned up. Fine glasspaper held on a cork rubber can be used in the direction of the grain and will be all that is necessary. It is almost inevitable that a few places will call for attention, because it is only too easy to mistake a pencil line for the shadow of an edge when cutting, and such inaccuracies only come to light when the pencil marks are removed by the glasspapering. However, such marks should be kept to a minimum because the effect of using glasspaper is to leave abrasive granules in the grain which are bad for the cutting edges of tools.

Good practice. As an exercise to help you to achieve crisp, clean cutting so essential for lettering, try this on a piece of oak. Without marking out, stab the wood perpendicularly across the grain with a 19mm. (¾in.) chisel and mallet, then a slanting blow from the right and again one from the left to produce the V cut section. Try a dozen or two of these movements with a rhythm of 1, 2, 3.

Now on the ends of each V incision put serifs. Use the flat gouge already suggested but without mallet. Cut with a slicing movement, first on the right, then the left, linking these cuts with the central line of the already cut uprights. Finally cut the top to complete, keeping up the same rhythm as before. Do not rectify any false cuts made but rather make fresh efforts until good results have

Fig. 11 Cutting serif using narrow chisel. Size of panel is 0.35m. (13¾in.) by 0.31m. (12½in.). Letters are 31mm. (1¼in.) high.

Fig. 12 Second serif cut again using narrow chisel.

Fig. 13 The completed panel carved in oak.

been obtained. Apart from appreciating the progress made in your cutting, the right use of only two tools has an economic value.

Raised lettering. So far our concern and practice has been with the cutting of incised letters, the best to begin with and perhaps the most used for inscriptions in wood. In addition there is raised lettering to be cut, and the use of this depends a good deal on the position it is finally to occupy; also the cost, for, unlike the former surface work, all wood surrounding the letters has to be cleared to a required depth or grounded out, which of course takes considerably longer. It is, however, most effective, and more suited than the V section where light conditions are poor. In fact it becomes a carved panel in relief, and should not represent any difficulties if the instruction already given on grounding is carried out.

For technical reasons the letters are heavier in general structure, and, unlike the V section, are well suited for carving any way of the grain. The best section for general purposes is shown at Fig. 14B with slight slanting sides. The section never looks well if the sides are cut down perpendicular, and worse still if undercut. The serifs are generally small and blunt. Care has to be exercised in the setting down of the outline, particularly the curved sections, for these are seen and are an integral part of the letter. Make sure you have the right tools from the outset, in fact do not start until you have. Improvising with a wrong tool to get a right shape invariably leads to disaster and mistakes are not easily remedied. Thin spade chisels and

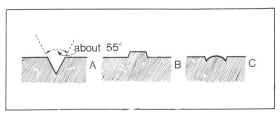

Fig. 14 Sections through various styles of letters: A Incised: B Raised: C Rounded and sunk.

Fig. 15 Decorative raised lettering book cover in pearwood. The tooling of the background adds interest.

103

gouges well sharpened inside and out are the best choice.

A woodcarver's router set to the required depth can be a great help for making the groundwork reasonably level. So too can a power-driven electric router save considerable time by going through the space between each line of lettering, and then with the help of grounders connect the spaces around each letter to the main groundwork. This need not necessarily be a perfectly smooth surface, but make an effort to make it so. The practice of frosting or punching the background is not recommended. It never looks well, and is often only a way of covering up faulty backgrounds. In any case it never enhances well cut letters in relief.

Raised lettering also looks well in stone and metal. The illustration in Fig. 16 was cut in pine first and subsequently cast in bronze. Never make the relief more than about one-third of the lower width of the perpendicular members. Fig. 14C looks very well in gold or colour, particularly if the gold leaf is burnished, provided you do not touch the slanting sides. There are other sections used, usually for larger work such as names on fascia boards and generally drawn, fretcut, and shaped as individual letters. They may be up to 0·60m. high, and are pinned, glued, or sometimes bolted to a backboard. Others are used in isolation with foliage as ciphers and monograms. Quite an interesting field of study, but outside the purview of this work.

Fig. 16 Panel with raised lettering and plaque in shallow relief. The entire thing was carved in wood and subsequently cast in bronze. Size of panel is 0.60m. (24in.) by 0.40m. (16in.) over-all.

Chapter seventeen

Carving in the round

This type of carving differs from what we have dealt with hitherto in that it has to be viewed from all sides as in a bust, animal, or figure carving, and in some elaborate ornament carvings. Clearly it poses many problems which do not occur in either work in the flat, or that which has a certain amount of modelling in depth.

The method followed by carvers varies considerably with the individual. Some use practically nothing but carving tools from beginning to end, feeling their way as the work progresses.

This is a subjective process, with the final result perceived from the outset. Probably it is a slow and uneconomic way judged by contemporary methods of working but nevertheless to some the only way. Others arrive at completion by continuous thought expressed in the first instance by careful studies and sketches, not only of the subject, but the final composition; never losing sight of the wood and dimensions already at hand.

Others do not hesitate to have the bulk of the unwanted wood removed on the bandsaw. This latter method applies particularly when a definite drawing of the work has been prepared, with its front and side elevations. This is not an easy method without an intimate knowledge of the subject. I find it best to prepare a small model, say a quarter full size of the final work. Assuming the finished work to be 0·60m. (24in.), let the model be in clay, Plasticine, or wax. By working on a small scale model one can see the limitations imposed by the material to be carved. Having completed the scale sketch but not in detail, prepare full size working drawings from it, particularly the front and side elevations, for from the outline of these the carving begins.

Since the precise over-all shape is known, the waste might just as well be removed by the easiest and quickest method, since there is no virtue in labour merely as such.

Removing waste on bandsaw. As an example of this, Fig. 1 represents the elevations and plan of a parakeet. Clearly all the wood outside the

(left) Bust in lime wood. Over-all height 0.37m. (15in.). Carved by Donald Wellman.

outline in both front and side elevations is **waste**, and can be sawn away first in front, then side, elevation, leaving a figure which is rectangular in plan section, and requiring the corners to be rounded. The advantage of the method, apart from its time and labour saving, is that there are four surfaces, all of which at some point represent the outer line of the figure.

One or two technical points have to be watched in following this method. The front and side elevations have to be marked out on adjacent faces as in Fig. 2, care being taken to position both at the same level, so that, say, the beak is at the same height in both. The front elevation is now cut on the band-saw, and wherever possible the waste pieces at each side are retained in a single piece. This is not always possible. In Fig. 3 for instance, there are two pieces at each side, but avoid cutting up the waste into several pieces. The reason for this will become obvious in the next stage, that of sawing the side elevation.

It is obvious that sawing the front elevation removes the marks on the side elevation. The waste pieces are, therefore, replaced and if necessary held with one or two nails driven into waste parts. Thus the side outline is replaced into position and, by replacing the waste at the other side, a flat surface is again restored which will lie flat upon the table of the bandsaw. Fig. 4 shows the work after these second cuts have been made, resulting in the square-sectioned piece shown in Fig. 5.

It should be noted that large work in the round approaching life size requires a well-considered plan in making up the bulk of timber required before carving, and the skill of a joiner is sometimes required to produce the bulk necessary. The joints may have to be slot-screw jointed, dowelled or bolted, and in the case of a large crucifix a hand-rail screw is necessary. Whatever it may be, they must be good joints, for there is nothing more exasperating while working in the round to see joints opening, and the irritating procedure of making good by fillers, which always seem to show however well done.

An alternative often mentioned is carving from the solid tree trunk. On the face of it this seems a good idea, but is never successful however long it has

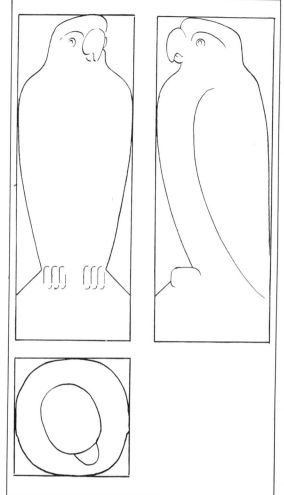

Fig. 1 Front and side elevations and plan of simple parakeet to be carved. The elevations should be drawn on adjacent faces of the wood block.

been seasoning. For whenever the heart of the tree is left, shakes of various kinds appear, and more so when the tree is opened up by tools in the different stages of carving. A close examination of some old work without shakes or cracks reveals that the wood was solidly jointed by joiners, but in a way that left the figure hollow. Sometimes, if not free

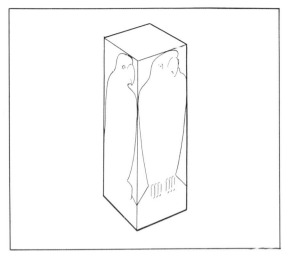

Fig. 2 The block marked out.

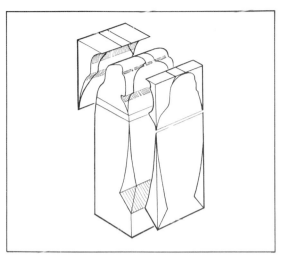

Fig. 4 Front elevation parts replaced and side elevation cut.

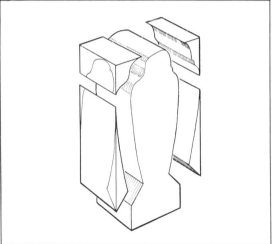

Fig. 3 Front elevation shape cut on bandsaw.

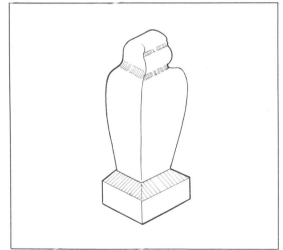

Fig. 5 The square section block after sawing.

standing but placed against a wall, this work was similarly hollowed, usually by the carver who wanted to make sure the heart was not there to destroy his work. In the Victoria and Albert Museum, London there are examples exemplifying this method. In the making up of larger work in the round which one knows will be subsequently gessoed, gilt, and coloured, this is usually built up in softwoods, with many parts in very high relief glued and tacked on. This is quite sound and if, prior to gilding, linen strips are put over the joints and faulty spots as explained in the chapter on gilding, all will be well and it will last for centuries as statuary of the mediaeval work has done.

Once the model has been completed it can be used

(Left) Angel carved in wood, and water gilt.
(Right) Figure in oak. Both carved by William
Wheeler.

to enable points to be measured off, thicknesses checked, and so on. Many carvers, however, keep and use this model up to the bosting-in stage only. Once this has been reached, the model is scrapped so that the carver can concentrate entirely upon the carving. Another point about the model is that it must be thought of in terms of wood. Thin, delicate detail is clearly undesirable and often impossible.

In much small and some reasonably large work in the round today the finish is left from the tool, or finished up to a degree of burnishing to enhance a specific wood and its grain. Those who favour this form of treatment should try to eliminate joins in the wood. If absolutely necessary the minimum should be used and these well away from the chief points of interest. Otherwise it destroys the aesthetic interest of wood sculpture, particularly when odd bits are stuck on to give additional relief, like features of the face.

When large work is made up ready for carving and much of the waste has been cleared away by the bandsaw, it can be extremely heavy and awkward to handle in the initial stages, and by far the best way to overcome this, after saw cuts have been made to further assist clearing the waste, is to put the work on the floor. Then with an adze and a blade shaped roughly to the curvature of a No. 3 or 4 gouge, and a width of approximately 50mm. (2in.), bost the work in, pushing the work from side to side occasionally with the foot. If a foot is placed at each side of the work, accidents are less likely to happen with the adze. Clear away at this stage as much of the wood as possible. Unless some quick method is adopted as here suggested to clear away the bulk of waste, the task can be tiresome before the actual finishing commences.

Nearly all the bosting-in of large work is done with large gouges and mallet. Where practicable the cut is across the grain as it is generally easier and less liable to split. Sometimes, when the bulk of the wood has been removed, it is a help to continue with a large rasp or shaper tool, especially on rounded surfaces. These tools when used with discretion enable one to get good shapes and lines without lumpiness quicker in some modelling than gouge work.

Viewing the work. In all work of this kind get into the habit of looking at it from all angles, and

Fig. 7 Vigorous horse head in elm. Carved by Thomas Brookbank.

keep in mind the position in which the figure will eventually be fixed. It might, for instance, have to stand on a high pedestal or whatever it might be, and clearly this has to be taken into account. The woodcarver's stand is a help in that one can walk all round it and observe it from all angles.

Another point to remember is that of the lighting it may eventually have. If possible this should be reproduced in the studio. Otherwise a trick of lighting may give an unforseen effect. This, however, applies only to large work to be in a fixed position.

When a carving follows a model it is necessary to fix on one or two datum points from which measurements can be taken. Otherwise there is nothing from which to measure. If such points are fixed at the outset in both model and carving it is simple to mark off other positions from such points, using calipers, dividers, and other measuring appliances. If an exact replica in wood has to be made from a plaster cast a pointing instrument has to be used. Obviously, when more than one datum point is used they must be in exact relation in both model and wood, and they must not be cut away until the work is so advanced as to make their retention unnecessary.

Chapter eighteen

Carving in the round — Eagle

The bird in Fig. 1 is painted in natural colours, one advantage of which is that almost any wood can be used. Those who prefer, however, could carve it in hardwood such as oak or teak and leave it in natural colour.

A block of wood to finish 0·33m. × 131mm. × 100mm. (13in. × 5in. × 4in.) is needed for Fig. 1. It could, however, be made larger or smaller as required. Instead of taking the squares in Figs. 2–4 as representing 25mm. (1in.) they could be 19mm. ($\frac{3}{4}$in.) or 31mm. (1$\frac{1}{4}$in.) the over-all sizes being adapted accordingly. Avoid too small a carving as it is difficult to put in the detail.

Drawing. A full size drawing is needed first, front and side elevation. Rule up a series of squares as in Figs. 2 and 4 and plot in the shape map fashion. The main outline is needed chiefly, but a certain amount of detail—eyes, beak, head shape, etc., should be put in so that their positions can be plotted later.

Prepare a block of wood, and plane to the finished over-all size. Note from Fig. 4 that the beak projects beyond the block. It is much simpler to glue on a piece later rather than have a thick block and have to reduce it. This is dealt with later. For the present the beak is ignored.

Preliminary cutting to shape. To mark out the shape cut out a thin cardboard template of the outline of the front shape (Fig. 4), and, holding this on the wood, draw round the outline. It is a help if the same shape is drawn on the back, the template being reversed so that the bird is facing the same way. This repeat of the outline on the back is a help when cutting the shape, as it marks the limit and enables the shape to be cut from both back and front. When a bandsaw is available it is unnecessary.

To remove the waste make a series of saw cuts across the grain down to just short of the line, and chop away the waste wood with chisel and gouge. This will produce the approximate outline as seen from the front.

Fig. 1 *(left)* Naturalistic eagle finished in colours. The bird is the South American crested eagle. It is 0.33m. (13in.) high. Carved by Charles H. Hayward.

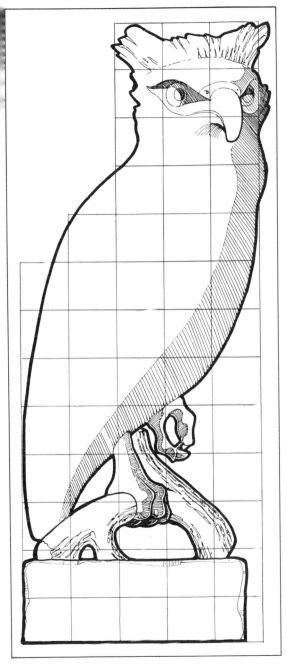

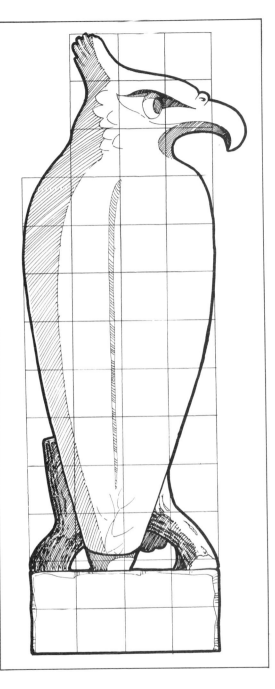

Fig. 2 Side elevation. The squares represent 25mm. (1in.) each.

Fig. 3 Back view.

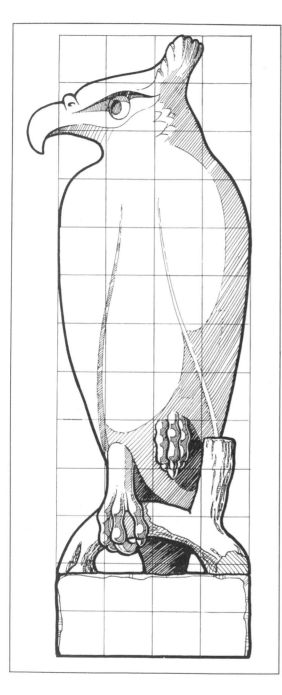

Fig. 4 Front elevation

The **side** elevation has now to be put in, **and it is** clearly necessary to draw on the undulating surface. The simplest way is to measure in from the edge and the top the position of certain points, and join these up to form a continuous line. Repeat the same points on the back so that the work can be tackled from both front and back.

Once again saw across the grain and chisel away the waste. If the chisel is taken inwards from the edges there will be no tendency to split out the corners. This will produce the shape shown in Fig. 5. It gives the roughly correct elevations, side and front, but is necessarily square in section. This preliminary squaring in is most desirable since, apart from giving the approximately correct shape, side and front, it enables measurements to be taken.

Bosting-in. The general rounding of the body, shaping of the head, rough positioning of the legs and tree trunk now follow. Generally it is simpler and conducive to a good shape if the gouging is done across the grain as shown in Fig. 6. Note that the head is turned sideways, though not quite at right angles, and the pitch of this in plan should be put in. It has obviously to blend comfortably into the body, and this is done at this stage.

Look at the work from all angles and try to produce good sweeping curves. The gouge marks can be ignored at present, the important point being to produce a shape which is approximately right in main form. The general fault of men doing the job for the first time is that they tend to make the section too square. Remember, then, that the bosting is more than the mere removal of the corners. Use a fairly large, half-round gouge for the purpose. One of 16mm. ($\frac{5}{8}$in.) or so is about right. Working across the grain is of special value in avoiding the square effect, and it largely avoids splitting the corners.

It will be realised that towards the base there is no question of rounding. Instead, the tree branch has to be formed, this running approximately from corner to corner. Cut away the waste wood so that the general direction of the bough is formed, and leave it full so that there is sufficient wood for the claws. Leave a chunk for the right foot on the bough, and another chunk higher up in which the left foot can be carved. Fig. 6 shows the idea. At present there is no need to pierce right through to

Fig. 5 The block after being cut on the bandsaw.

Fig. 6 Early stage in bosting-in with gouges.

form the legs, but depressions can be made so that the position of the parts is obvious.

When the head has been brought reasonably to shape at the correct angle, and the neck made to blend into both head and body, a flat surface can be cut with the chisel to enable a block to be glued on from which the beak will be carved. When the glue has set the curved side view can be cut in and the taper towards the tip formed. In the actual bird the beak is considerably thinner, but, since the carving is in wood, it is advisable to keep it fairly thick. Another detail in which the carving must necessarily vary from the original is that the crested feathers at the back of the head must remain reasonably thick. In the bird, of course, they are thin. This is a typical convention that one accepts.

Modelling. The detail modelling is now put in without the final detail itself being carved. For instance, the deep depressions for the eyes are cut, leaving sufficient wood for the eyes themselves. Note that these eyes face the front, not the side as in the case of, say, a duck. It is a help if the curve formed by the brow is cut in on the underside with V tool or narrow U tool. The depression is particularly marked between the front of the eye itself and the beak. Since the eye is square with the front, the depression behind it is far less. Finish the eye to its rounded shape as smooth as you can, holding the gouge concave side downwards. The same thing applies to the beak.

The rest of the bird, however, can show tool facets as these help to suggest feathers. To this end work the gouge in the direction the feathers would take up. Use a flat gouge for all rounded parts. On the back and breast the facets can be quite marked, but on the top of the head they should be much smaller, as in the bird itself the feathers here would be smaller and the general surface smoother.

Legs. The work of piercing the wood to separate the leg and tree bough requires patience and care.

A small front-bent gouge is extremely useful for reaching into the awkward parts—in fact it may be a necessity for some detail. When the main form has been brought to shape the bark can be put in with veiner or V tool.

To form the claws cut the foot to the main over-all shape and separate the claws by making a cut between them with a small veiner. This clears much of the waste and enables a small, fairly flat gouge to be stabbed in to form the knuckle shape. The markings on the legs and claws are merely coloured, and are not carved in.

In all the carving the main guiding rules to follow are: complete the general shaping or bosting before putting in detail. Follow the grain of the wood in the final stages to avoid splitting the grain. Keep the tools razor-sharp, especially when finishing off.

Finishing. If the bird is to be in natural wood it can be left as it is or finished with wax. If paint is preferred it can either be finished with artists' oil colours, or treated with poster water colours, then varnished. Poster colours cover well and are quite opaque. Furthermore they dry rapidly. Chief colours are: Body black to grey, feathers occasionally verging to white. Beak slate blue. Eyes middle brown with black pupils. Depression in front of eyes yellow with blue-grey markings. Legs and claws pasty yellow with black markings. Talons black.

The bird is the South American crested eagle and is taken from one in the Natural History Museum, in London.

Chapter nineteen

Gilding—tools

Generally speaking, the craft of gilding appears to run parallel with life. The origins of it, whether it be the tools, materials, processes, or its application are quite unknown to us. More than that, it is substantially the same whatever part of the world one visits today. In Egypt as far back as 3000 B.C. we have records of processes and materials and their preparation which for the most part correspond with those employed by the gilder of today. The durability of water gilding under normal conditions appears to have no time factor at all. Water gilding covers the couch at Luxor on which Tutankhamun rested, and the burnished head which adorns one end is as perfect today as when it was done 3000 years ago.

The gilder of today can still with pride give the same guarantee of durability. Unlike other forms of embellishment, gilding never varies with fashion, whether it be association with architectural enrichment or the decoration of furniture. It makes little difference if the gilding is on wood or stone, leather, or vellum; used in tempera painting seen in galleries throughout the world, on ikons of the Russian Church, or some of the fine picture frames in an art museum—the technique of the craft is fundamentally the same.

Whatever one tries to introduce in the way of new materials or processes in an effort to bring it into line with contemporary thought and economic working, there is nothing which will prove more worthy and lasting than the methods which have stood the test of centuries. It is these which it is proposed to give in the following pages.

Preparation of gold leaf. Before proceeding further let us have a general picture of how gold leaf is prepared before it reaches the gilder in the convenient form of tissue books. Like the technique of using gold leaf, that of making the leaf is also traditional. We read of the processes of 4000 years ago, and we know, as far as the size and weight of each leaf is concerned, it is for all intents and purposes the same today. As a point of interest, there are in the Louvre, Paris, leaves of gold found among Egyptian remains which on examination were found to be a little thicker than those which are used today. It may be that the 8lb. hammer now

Fig. 1 *(left)* Mirror or frame in carved pine and water gilt by Clifford Wright.

in use for working the moulds is of steel, not bronze, which was the custom of the Egyptian goldbeater that has made the difference.

The gold after being melted in a crucible is cast in slabs of 150mm. × 25mm. × 3mm. From this stage the ingots go continuously through rollers of steel. From time to time increased pressure is put on the rollers, and after much annealing, the ingots are now transformed into strips of gold approximately 31mm. wide and 0·0025mm. thick. This is as far as the mechanical process can go, and from this stage to the end of the task of beating the gold to a thickness of 0·00001mm. is all the hand work of craftsmen, who by their cunning enable other craftsmen to further embellish their own craft.

The strips of gold are now cut into 25mm. (1in.) squares, and carefully placed between leaves of vellum about 100m. (4in.) square, known as a 'cutch'. Some 200 leaves are used at a time in this process, and bound together by bands of parchment. Then the hand beating with a 20lb. steel hammer takes place, until the precious metal spreads out to the 100mm. vellum squares. This operation takes about half an hour.

The gold is now taken from the 'cutch', cut into four by a knife (skewing), each quarter being placed between skins of about 113mm. (4½in.) square. Eight hundred skins are used at a time, and the bundle, called a 'shoder', is ready for the next beating, but this time with a 12lb. hammer. As with 'cutch', the leaves spread out just beyond the skins, are taken out, and quartered again by cutting.

Each quarter is now placed between further pieces of skin (in this case gold beaters' skin) of 131mm. square. For this operation 1000 skins at a time are used and is called a 'mould'. This is beaten for about five hours, thrusting the blows at the centre with an 8lb. hammer on a bench of solid marble until the precious metal spreads outwards. Free from cracks, small holes, and other blemishes or faults—a skilful task. These are then cut to size (81mm. (3¼in.) square) by a sharpened reed called a 'wagon' on a skin cushion, and placed leaf by leaf—by hand and the help of boxwood pincers—into the thin paper books consisting of 25 leaves. One hundred books are termed a pack.

The various shades of colour available, from white

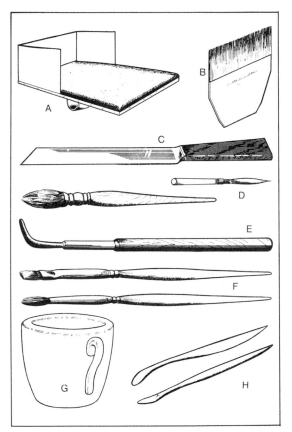

Fig. 2 Tools used in gilding.

to red, are caused by the addition of small quantities of copper or silver as an alloy in the early stages of manufacture. An alloy, too, is necessary during the constant beating of gold; without it the material would crack. Much of the gold treasure taken by the British in the Punjab split whilst being marked as the gold was too pure.

Tools used in gilding. As with the craft of woodcarving, let us begin with the tools. These are neither numerous nor expensive and all are available today, see Fig. 2.

A *Gilder's cushion.* Could be made at home. It is a piece of softwood 200mm. × 140mm. × 13mm. (8in. × 5½in. × ½in.) usually clamped to prevent warping. It is first covered with three thicknesses of fine flannel. Stretched over these is a soft chamois wood. At one end and partly round two sides is a windscreen or wall of parchment about 75mm. (3in.) high made to fold flat when not in use. The sides when raised shelter the gold while working, for the slightest draught will lift the gold from the cushion, and it is an almost impossible task to recapture it from the floor or elsewhere, because of its thinness. On the underside of the cushion is a loop of leather for the thumb. This enables the cushion to be held like a palette when in use.

B *Gilder's tip.* Made in various widths, and consisting of hairs sandwiched between two pieces of thin cardboard. They are used to pick up the gold from the cushion prior to being placed on the surface to be gilded.

C *Gilder's knife.* With square handle, well balanced. It has a fairly flexible blade, not very sharp, and is used for cutting the single sheets of gold when on the cushion into sizes convenient for the job on hand.

D *Gilder's mop.* No. 3 camel hair (a quill with a wooden handle). A liner of sable or quill about 38mm. (1½in.) long can be slipped on the end of the mop and used for pressing home the gold immediately it has been laid in water.

E *Burnishers.* Made of agate or flint. Must be highly polished to prevent scratching or cutting the gold. The stones are best set on wooden handles. Some are being produced today on metal handles which become uncomfortable after hours of burnishing. Two burnishers are enough for most work.

F *Brushes.* A number of hog hair brushes (round and flat) of artist's quality for putting on gesso or similar operations. The handles are best shortened by cutting in half for the gilder's use. Sable and camel hair brushes of various sizes, sometimes called pencils, are also frequently used.

G *Pipkins.* These are earthenware pots, glazed inside, about 125mm. (4in.) diameter at top, with handles. Use for preparing size and making up gesso, etc. They are difficult to get these days. A good alternative is to use a double saucepan or porringer, or the water section of a glue pot in which could be placed an earthenware jar.

H *Modellers.* Of metal and wood of various shapes, and improvised ones made from toothbrush handles, are used for shaping up ornaments in gesso or compo, either when originally applied, or making replacements.

Materials.
1 Parchment cuttings or rabbit skin. Both easily obtainable and inexpensive. Parchment size is a little more complicated to make up but, generally speaking, gives better results.

2 Gilder's whiting. This is more refined and less gritty than builder's or household whiting. The finest is slaked plaster of Paris.

3 Oil gold size normally called 18-hour gold size. That is the time it takes roughly to become tacky and ready for the gold to be laid. For exterior work, or work with paint undercoating, a quick-drying size is used. Japan gold size is usually used and goes off in about an hour.

4 Yellow clay, matt gold size, burnish gold size and blue burnish. These preparations are bought in paste form, then size (parchment) is added and mixed to a consistency of thin cream. Put on after gesso is laid and before gilding takes place. Depending on the ultimate effect of the gilding, one or all of the preparations mentioned can be used on the same job.

5 Gilder's Ormulu. This gives oil or matt gilding a richer and deeper colour, and forms a wonderful contrast to burnished water gilding. Ormulu is generally mixed with parchment size before use. For the protection of gilding after completion a colourless gold lacquer is sometimes used.

6 Gold Leaf. This is sold in books, with 25 leaves in each book, termed loose leaf or transfer. The former, as the name indicates, is free and placed on a cushion for subsequent cutting. The transfer is the same gold as the loose, i.e. 25 sheets, except that each leaf is attached to tissue paper by a film of wax for easy handling for oil gilding, particularly for outside work.

All the tools and materials mentioned above can be obtained from an artists' colourman.

Chapter twenty

Gilding—the practical work

Fig. 1 Section and detail of frame in Fig. 2

The illustration of the carved mirror frame in Fig. 2 is given as an example to cover two methods of gilding, both oil and water, at the same time introducing the simple diaper patterns impressed in the gesso ground often seen in the backgrounds and draperies of tempera paintings as well as frames. In addition it exemplifies the toning of gold.

The carving. To begin with the frame is made up with a moulding of rounds and hollows and some carving in relief. The material may be of pine, mahogany, lime, or walnut, not oak. The latter is not suitable as its open grain will not give that richness and sparkle which gilding demands. For those who wish to make the frame illustrated, a section is given in Fig. 1. The over-all size is 0·48m. × 0·36m. (19in. × 14¼in.).

The carving has a relief of about 6mm. (¼in.); that is at the mitres and the central pattern in the centre of each side. Carving the berry and sausage moulding and the ribbon pattern is governed as far as relief is concerned by the sections. Generally speaking the modelling for carving to be gilded should be broad and soft in character, without deep V tool or veiner treatment, and avoiding undercutting as far as possible, as all these tend to be over-clogged with gesso.

Gesso preparation. The first task is to prepare the size for the gesso foundation. Obtain some parchment cuttings (goat or sheep), cut up into pieces an inch or two long, well cover with water, and leave overnight. In the morning throw the water away, transfer the cuttings to the inner part of a double kettle, and add water roughly three times the volume of the cuttings. The outer saucepan is filled with hot water and kept at simmering point for three or four hours. By then nearly all the cuttings will have disappeared.

Strain through a fine mesh strainer or odd bit of nylon stocking into a pipkin or jar, and return the remnants to the saucepan for further use. Let the strained size cool and coagulate. It is only when in this condition that the strength of size can be judged for the various gilding operations. For the beginner it is a matter of trial and error. If, when the size is cold, you can push your finger into it without its breaking apart, and it has a springy tenacity, it is too strong. The size is also too strong if on striking the pipkin two or three times with the

Fig. 2 Mirror frame in wood and water gilt.
Carved by William Wheeler.

palm of hand there is no visible sign of disintegrating. In this case add a little water, warm up, cool and try again. When the size shatters under the same tests or is comparable to a nicely made fruit jelly, it is about right to use.

Now warm up again, add gilder's whiting, and mix well together with a piece of wood or blunt table knife, pressing out lumps against the body of the pipkin until all is like a consistency of ready-mixed paint. Add two drops of linseed oil or a little Russian tallow (about the size of a pea) and stir well. Warm up and stir and it is now ready for use.

Applying gesso. With a hog-hair brush, preferably a flat one, carefully put on the first coat. This is sometimes called the thin white. Keep the container in the hot water pan to prevent it from jelling whilst working. Now follow 6 to 8 coats until a good foundation has been built up.

Remember the following points which are the result of experience. Always make sufficient size to cover the eight coats. Though each coat must be dry before the next is laid, all coats must be completed in one day. Artificial drying by a fire or on top of a radiator is not recommended, either for the wood or the gesso.

Remember if too strong a size is used the gesso is apt to flake off, and if too weak the gesso may powder off. Where knots and joints (particularly at mitres) occur in a job, take fine linen or silk, cut up in pieces which will well cover the area, and before the second coat is applied, dip the silk into gesso and stretch it over those parts that are inclined to open or move. On this build up the subsequent layers.

Do not rub down with glasspaper between each coat. The last two or three coats when taken from the pipkin are inclined to be thick. To remedy add a little water, not size. This is a good point to remember. If by accident the size or gesso boils throw it out, for it creates bubbles and other complications not easily overcome.

In applying the many coats be sure that they cover effectively, because there is often a tendency to form little bridges over recessed parts which when dry crack and break. For correcting pin holes and small defects, mix together a little whiting and size to the consistency of putty and use as a filler.

Alternative size. Before proceeding to the next stage, here is an alternative to parchment cuttings for size. This is rabbit skin purchased at suppliers of gilder's materials. It is in the form of sheets of gelatine but is darker in colour. To prepare take one sheet, break it up into pieces, put in a pipkin, and cover with cold water. After a few hours' soaking it is warmed up in a glue kettle. Then adopt the same procedure as for parchment size. It is quicker to prepare and there is little difference in using. Both take a good burnish.

As an alternative to gilder's whiting, mention must be made of slaked plaster of Paris. Get the fine quality, say a 7lb. bag, and put into a pan or tub. Add plenty of water (about 1 gallon to every pound of plaster), stir it frequently for a while, then every day for several days. It is as well to renew the water occasionally. It will now be found that all the fiery heat has gone, and it is completely slaked. Leave for three or four weeks. Take it from the container, put it into a piece of rag, and squeeze all water from it. It is made into cakes until required, and used with parchment size as directed for gilder's whiting. Under the microscopic slaked plaster of Paris shows long thread-like crystals matted together, whereas whiting shows crystals that are nearly cube shaped. When applied to the work the ground receives the burnishing much better than the whiting, and was the only method used for centuries all over the world both for water gilding or the grounds for tempera painting, or the combination of both.

Importance of a good gesso foundation. To ensure a complete mixing with the size it is not a bad plan to work the gesso through a hair sieve. If the eight coats, or less according to the nature of the work, are perfectly laid, nothing needs to be done to the final coat. But this seldom happens to beginners. However, you must realise from the outset that the ground now prepared is primarily for receiving gold leaf which in turn has to be burnished with stone. Nothing must be left on the ground that would irritate or tear the gold, which, it will be remembered, is only 1/250,000 part of an inch thick. The surface, therefore, has to be extremely smooth. Gesso, by its nature, cannot be otherwise if properly prepared.

Applying it is not always successful. Sometimes the surface is rough and much more uneven than anticipated. So, using No. 0 or flour glasspaper, gently rub the affected parts to get a smooth surface. The glasspaper should just slightly cut the gesso. If it is found, say, in some of the hollows and other parts, that too much gesso has come to rest, you can easily clean by using an old piece of linen dipped in water, squeezing out, and wrapped round various shaped modelling tools, or shaped-up pieces of wood to suit the contour. Like using glasspaper, this has to be very carefully done, bearing in mind that the gesso surface must be retained.

There is a school of thought which suggests that at this stage the whole should be recut by carving tools to conform with the modelling of the carving beneath. This will, of course, sharpen up the outlines and contours, but will certainly not enhance the quality of water gilding. So if the gesso preparation appears to have slightly rounded off the forms leave it, for a better metallic result will be obtained in the final burnishing.

Application of bole. The next stage is covering the surface with Armenian bole. This is an earth, red in colour, which, with the addition of size, can be bought ready for use. It is not difficult to make, and some gilders prefer to make their own by mixing 'pure' bole in its raw state with an equal quantity of pipe clay and water mixed into a thick paste with palette knife on a glass palette. In addition to the red, you can buy yellow clay, matt burnish, and blue burnish. The latter contains graphite and gives an unusually bright burnish. All the clays can be intermixed to obtain a colour to suit the particular tone, or the style of work required. It is not proposed to go into the quantities used for special jobs, as experience alone can produce this, particularly the antique gold known as 'distressing'. So for the time being let us keep to bole for water gilding and yellow clay for oil gilding.

For the application take some warm parchment size, add the prepared bole, and mix to a consistency of thin cream, making sure that it is a good mix by straining through a small mesh strainer. Remember, too, the strength of size for this preparation is half that used for the making of gesso. Make sufficient for three or four coats to ensure having the same strength of size throughout.

The first coat should be put on with a hog-hair brush, and the remainder with camel-hair. Let each coat dry before proceeding with the next. It is the practice of some gilders to put the first coat on thin (i.e. with little bole) and for each subsequent coat to add a little more bole. In any case, when the last coat is completed and dry, the whole job has the appearance of having been painted with a dark red matt paint, with no sign of the white gesso beneath. In applying the bole there is a tendency for ridges to be formed. The use of the camel-hair brushes will help to guard against this. Leave to dry overnight, and it is as well to cover the job over to prevent picking up dust, etc.

Cennino Cennini, in his treatise on gilding, suggests mixing the bole with beaten white of egg. First extract the white, put in a glass or basin, beat up to a thick froth, and leave overnight to clarify itself. Pour on the same amount of water, add the bole, and proceed as for bole mixed with size. There is little in it, except that the white of egg preparation is less affected by damp. It is possible to buy French burnishing clay, made up in little cones, which contains the white of egg in the manufacture and is found extremely useful when small quantities are required. All that is needed is to rub a wet camel-hair brush on the cone and then paint on the job. It is particularly suitable for small repair jobs.

Final preparation. Now with a piece of linen rag, burnish up the bole with great care. Maybe before this is done there are found to be specks or nibs of

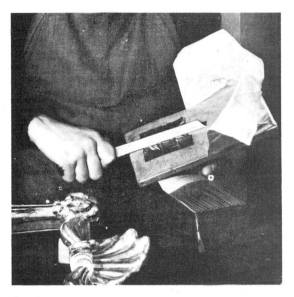

Fig. 3 Cutting gold leaf on the cushion.

bole on the surface like tops of small pins. Remove these first with No. 0 glasspaper, rubbed together first to prevent cutting too much away. The result should be a highly polished dark red surface. It is as well at this stage always to cover up the job when not actually working on it, for foreign bodies like dust and grit, however small, can play havoc whether before or after the burnishing.

Handling gold leaf. In the next stage have by you the cushion page 116, Fig. 2A, the tip Fig. 2B, the knife Fig. 2C, camel-hair mop with the liner Fig. 2D slipped on the end, and book of gold (loose leaf). Have also a pipkin or cup of clean water into which is placed one tablespoon of parchment size as prepared for the gesso. Hold cushion in the left hand with the thumb in the loop and the parchment screen up. Open the book of gold, and with the aid of the knife, pass a leaf on to the cushion. Manipulate it until it is reasonably flat. Breathe on it, and, if all goes well, it should be flat as if attached to the cushion.

Do not breathe on the knife for it is apt to pick up the gold leaf. To prevent this lightly rub the knife with No. 0 glasspaper occasionally. Do not blow the leaf on the cushion, for it will soon disappear if you do, and is not easy to recover. Now with knife in right hand, cut the leaf with whole edge of knife (which should not be too sharp). Lay down the knife, and pass the tip (in the same hand) over the head or side of face swiftly two or three times. This will enable it to pick up the cut pieces of leaf easily with the edge of tip. Hold this with thumb and finger underneath the cushion.

Applying gold leaf. Now dip the mop into the prepared water, and well moisten that portion of the job which is to be covered with the cut piece of gold leaf. Then with great speed pick up the latter and float on to the surface, pressing home with liner now on the end of the mop. Some gilders prefer to use the hair of the tip itself. If the latter is used make sure that it does not get wet, for complications can arise in picking up the gold from the cushion, and damping the surface of the gold laid on the job. Furthermore the tip becomes untidy, with odd pieces of gold sticking to it, which does not help laying the gold.

Fig. 4 Transferring gold leaf to work with tip.

The first effort in laying gold will not be encouraging, but, though the procedure given above may seem difficult, practice will give perfection. It is amazing the number of books of gold a gilder can lay in the working day. The following should help in both good and speedy laying. Keep the windows and doors closed while working. This keeps the leaf on the cushion safe from movement. Cut up the gold economically; for instance, the pieces required for the ribbon moulding in Fig. 1 will be larger than those for the berry moulding. For the rest of the frame the larger the pieces the better. You will find that after some practice it will not be difficult to pick and lay half a leaf.

Try to avoid forming bridges with the gold, but rather wrap the gold round each bit of relief. You will find, too, that if the work is not wet enough the gold will not adhere; on the other hand, too wet a surface will stain the gold, and turn it a yellow colour which is impossible to burnish. Try to make a good joint of the several pieces by not letting the size water touch the gold already laid. If there is an overlap, breathe on it well and quickly push home with tip or liner or even a little cotton wool.

Burnishing. Now comes the burnishing, and the tool for this is illustrated at Fig. 2E, page 116. When to start is for the most part governed by the atmospheric conditions of the room in which you

are working. After an hour or so try burnishing by first rubbing the burnisher on your coat to clean and warm it, and then let the burnisher travel to and fro very softly over a small area, first by the weight of burnisher alone, and then slightly increase the pressure. In a minute or so a noticeable gloss should be seen. If not, leave for a while and try again. This might be called a temperamental stage and has to be humoured; it certainly cannot be forced. Damp and mild weather seems better for burnishing than, say, the dry summer weather, but this must not be taken too literally, though it be true. Anyway, a dampish place is certainly better than a very dry place to stand the work while waiting to be burnished.

It is not a sound practice to leave the burnishing too long after the laying of the bole. A day or so but not longer, for the ground becomes hard and doesn't take kindly to burnishing. If for some reason you cannot tackle the actual burnishing for three or four weeks, try this. Take a handkerchief and place it over the job requiring burnishing. Take another handkerchief, wet it well with clean water, wring it out as dry as you can by hand, and place over the dry one. In an hour or less, depending on the time of the year, the work will be ready for the stone again.

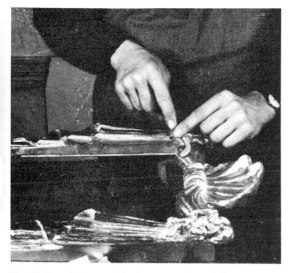

Fig. 5 Burnishing with the agate burnisher.

You will already have discovered that the high and rounder forms become brightest under the burnisher. This is as it should be. Do not try to burnish spots where even the smallest stone cannot reach; let these areas remain matt. It is the contrast of matt and burnished surfaces which enhances the work. In fact, the gilder usually works out a scheme of different finishes before he begins the job. To emphasise the matt surfaces the usual practice is to give the surface a very weak coat of parchment size to which is added a tablespoon of ormulu to a cup of size. This, too, is the surface one must have if colour is to be introduced on the gilded surface.

After the gold has been laid, and just prior to burnishing, there will be spots of red showing through bad laying. The majority should be covered with gold and is known as faulting. The quickest way to remedy it is to pick odd bits of gold with the point of a sable brush, spot with the sized water and then lay the gold, breathe heavily on the spot and slightly push home with cotton wool. The breathing helps to amalgamate the surfaces not touched with water, and the burnishing will do the rest.

Protective coating. Normally the burnished surfaces of work needs no protection in the majority of cases. Sometimes, however, there is need for surface protection where the work is handled, such as caskets, altar candlesticks, etc. A coat of fine silver varnish, or a cellulose lacquer will protect without noticeably affecting the lustre.

Tool patterns. The diaper pattern on the large curved moulding of the frame is produced by indenting with home made, very blunt metal or wood tools shaped to fit the pattern, the dots being formed with a stylo. Make sure of your pattern first by making a template of the section of the moulding, and mark out the diapers in pencil. Press the tool into the paper to get a little practice as well as to view the completed pattern. When satisfied proceed to give the same pattern on the burnished gold moulding. In doing so care must be exercised not to mark the surface by tracing with carbon paper, and pencils. This is definitely a free-hand effort, but with the aid of dividers and the edge of a piece of notepaper to guide the straight members it does not present a great difficulty.

Try the dots first, by pressing the stylo perpendicularly into the gold. If well done it makes a dot indentation without cutting the gold or gesso. If you do see the occasional speck of red bole, leave it, as it can add a little interest. Proceed with the other patterns, using of course the tools you previously made.

The little dark flowers in the centre of each main diamond are burnished, and to enhance them go over the remainder of the diaper pattern with thin parchment size plus a tablespoon of ormulu in say a cupful of size. This indeed gives a remarkable sparkling and scintillating brightness. The possibilities are endless. Fine lettering can be done this way, by indenting (or engraving—as it is sometimes called) the outline. When complete, go over the background with the size and leave the lettering burnished. It is worth while going to an art museum just to see how this method is applied to tempera pictures and frames alike. When work is properly burnished 'the gold will appear almost dark from its own brightness' says Cennino Cennini.

Oil gilding. So far our efforts have been confined to achieving this brightness which only burnished water gilding can give. Now for oil gilding. The gilder who has to use this method, perhaps for economic reasons, would prepare the ground as for water gilding, using only two or three coats of gesso to fill the grain. This should be followed by a coat of yellow clay mixed as for Armenian bole. If necessary use No. 0 glasspaper, followed by two coats of clear size. A coat of gold size must now follow, and this is bought in small tins ready for use and usually termed 18-hour gold size, referring of course to the approximate time it will take to become tacky or ready to receive the gold. It is similar in colour to the yellow clay. The colour intensifies the effect of oil gilding, as the red bole does to water gilding.

Stir the size well, and with a flat hog brush (size of brush depends on job) go over the surface thoroughly, making sure all is covered. Make doubly sure that the surface is covered by the minimum amount of gold size. This must be stressed, for any suggestion of a puddle in the hollows or surplus on the higher parts will cause uneven dryouts. Furthermore, if the gold leaf is put on such surfaces it would never be permanent. Cover up the work after carefully sizing to prevent dust sticking, and from time to time test for tackiness by touching the gold size lightly with the finger, until it almost holds the finger in position. The drier the better.

Now cut the leaf on the cushion as for water gilding, apply with tip, and press down a little with the help of cotton wool wrapped in a piece of well-worn linen. Alternatively use transfer gold and press down with the same dabber. In small, difficult, and awkward spots press home with the help of modelling tools of varying shapes. It should be mentioned here that a gesso foundation is not vital for oil gilding, bearing in mind that you cannot burnish oil gilding, though it always looks better on a gesso ground. As an alternative ground, prepare the wood with paint priming. Give two or three undercoats until all sign of grain has disappeared, smooth down well with glass paper and finally give a coat of gloss paint, the finished colour being approximately that of the yellow clay. Having satisfied yourself that the surface is smooth and free from embedded specks of dust which would irritate the leaf, apply the gold size and gild.

For external work like fascia boards with large lettering, signs, etc., prepare with paint as above, but use Japan gold size which goes off tacky in about half an hour, very necessary when working outside. Always use transfer gold for outside work. No protection in the way of varnishes is necessary for the protection of the gold from the elements. But should it appear dirty after a year or so, carefully dust without scratching, then wash with a clean sponge and warm water only and let it dry without assistance.

Gilding lettering. It is as well to mention at this stage the usual method of gilding letters as shown on page 103. There are several ways depending on sections, material, and cost. If gilding incised lettering in oak, you may give each incision a coat of shellac (french polish), followed by gold size. Transfer gold is pressed home with fingers and the help of modelling tools. If the letters are cleanly cut it should suffice providing you do not mind the grain weeping through after a while. Better results are obtained if the grain is completely filled.

Oil paint is not so good for this, as the oil occasionally comes through at the top edges around the letters, and the leaf when applied adheres to the oily spots producing serrated lines where they should be straight. Cellulose and lacquer paints are much better to use. Remember that an obtuse rather than an acute angle looks better when gilt, apart from the fact that the leaf is easier to lay, and the dust does not settle so much in the incisions. Should odd bits of gold find their way onto the surface of panels or elsewhere they can easily be removed with indiarubber. Sections B and C, page 103 can be treated as for the V section A, providing the sides of section C are not gilt.

Burnished letters. To those who wish all letters burnished—and how well it looks!—here is a method which has proved highly successful, and it is worked on section C, page 103. First give the rounded surfaces of all letters one or two coats of hot size, the strength as used for the mixing of gesso. Now obtain red lead, *Lepage* glue, and casein size. Mix in a slant china palette with the help of a palette knife in the following way. Take a saltspoonful of red lead, add the least amount of water that will moisten it throughout. Add with a paint brush sufficient casein size to make a composition of workable consistency. Mix with palette knife. With tip of knife add a touch of *Lepage* glue, say half quantity of casein size, and mix again.

Never add water after mixing. If too little water, the composition will become too stiff to work after two or three letters have been laid. If too much water, the ground will be weak and will break into powder under the burnisher. If too much size and glue, the composition will remain in a puddle perhaps an hour after it has been laid. The red lead will sink to the bottom and the glue will harden over it, forming a scale which will chip off when burnished, leaving powdery red lead underneath. Casein size wants a lot of mixing. Add to it in the mixing ten drops of ammonia. A wad of cotton wool dipped in creosote pinned under the cork will keep it from going bad for three or four days.

In preparing the ground make sufficient to cover, say, fifteen 31mm. (1¼in.) letters at a time. When the mix is complete paint the letters with a sable brush. When dry it leaves a fine surface for the gold. Now lay the gold, preferably double thickness, with very weak white of egg or size. Watch your time and then burnish.

Royal Coat of Arms in English oak pierced and mounted on mahogany. Made by Anthony Steel.

Chapter twenty-one

Timbers for woodcarving

Several things have to be considered when selecting wood for carving. When appearance is of first importance, it may be a matter of matching other items, of picking an attractive or a plain grain, or of having a suitable colour. On the other hand, when the piece is to be painted or gilt the appearance of the wood does not matter much. Durability is obviously important in items to be exposed to the weather, and it has also to be reckoned with for things to be kept indoors in that some woods suffer more from woodworm than others. Size, too, comes into the picture, for miniature carvings need a close-grained hardwood, whereas big statuary, etc. must have a wood which can be obtained in reasonably large sizes. Lastly, from the purely technical angle, some woods carve much more happily than others, being crisp under the tool yet not unduly hard.

Often enough, it is a matter of compromise between these requirements. The following list gives the characteristics of woods which have been used in carving, together with their colour and weight. The last named is reckoned the air dry weight of a cubic foot of that timber, though it should be realised that there may be considerable variation since wood is a natural material. It is useful to have a general idea of weight, however, and the best way is to compare it with that of a known timber. For instance, most people have handled, say, oak, and if this is taken as a basis for comparison it is easy to form a good idea of the weight of some new wood with which one may not be familiar.

Lime (Tilia vulgaris). 37–38lb. Yellowish white colour, close-grained, with little grain marking. Carves beautifully, being firm and crisp without being unduly hard. Not specially durable, and may suffer from furniture beetle. Stands well when seasoned.

Walnut (Juglans regia). 40–46lb. Somewhat cold brown colour, fairly close-grained, often finely figured but is sometimes plain according to conversion. Carves well in every respect. Excellent for indoor items but liable to attack by furniture beetle. Stands well when seasoned. American black walnut is slightly lighter in weight and is not so richly figured, but is a fine carving wood.

Fig. 1 Angel carved in lime wood by Tilman Riemenschneider (early sixteenth century).

Mahogany, Honduras (Swietenia macrophylla). 34–39lb. Reddish brown colour, moderately close-grained. Figure varies widely from the extremely rich to the very plain. Carves well, especially the straight-grained varieties, but the grain of some can be tricky, sometimes with adjacent streaks of varying direction. Fine for indoor work and is immune from beetle attack. Stands well.

Mahogany, Cuban (Swietenia mahogoni). 40lb. Dark reddish brown with white chalky deposits in the pores. Figure varies from plain to richly marked. Harder than Honduras. Carves well and takes natural friction polish, but inclined to be brittle. Stands well. Difficult to obtain.

Mahogany, African (Khaya ivorensis). 30–40lb. according to variety. Reddish brown colour. Quality varies widely, sometimes woolly and open grained, and ranging from moderately hard to relatively soft. Some types carve well, others not so satisfactorily. Sometimes liable to twist in both length and across width.

Oak, English (Quercus robur). 45–52lb. Generally hard, but carves well. Open-grained which makes it unsuitable for delicate, miniature work. Durable and stands well when seasoned, but slash sawn boards are liable to warp. When quarter-cut the rich silver grain (rays) is exposed, this varying from large irregular markings to small flecks. Quarter-cut boards are the most reliable.

Pear (Pyrus communis). 47–48lb. Pale yellowish red. Excellent carving wood, having even texture and finishing smooth under the tool. Rather liable to twist unless carefully seasoned.

Oak, European. Similar characteristics to English oak, but generally the wood is milder.

Oak, Japanese (Quercus mongolica). Lighter than English oak but similar in appearance. Mild and rather more open-grained, but carves well, and keeps its shape when seasoned.

Sycamore (Acer pseudoplatanus). 38–39lb. Milk-white colour but turning a less pleasant yellow-brown shade on exposure. Obtainable in good sizes. Close-grained and fairly hard to carve. Stands well when seasoned.

Teak (Tectona grandis). 45lb. Cold yellow-brown shade, sometimes with black streaks. Coarse, open-grain, and greasy. Does not hold glue well. Carves well, and is excellent for outdoor work. Stands well.

Agba (Gossweilerodendron balsamiferum). 30lb. Yellowish pink to reddish brown colour. Medium-grain and fairly soft to cut. Carves well.

Pine. Varies tremendously according to species and quality. Best yellow pine *(Pinus strobus)* carves well but requires sharp tools with long bevels. Baltic pine *(Pinus sylvestris)* is not so satisfactory, the alternate layers of hard and soft grain making difficult working. Again keen tools are essential. Boards with knots should be avoided. Parana pine is unsuitable for carving.

Padauk (Pterocarpus dalbergioides). 54–59lb. Rich reddish colour, sometimes streaked with a darker colour. Tending to fade and darken on exposure. Rather open in grain and thus unsuitable for small, delicate work, but carves well though hard.

Dense hardwoods. These include such woods as ebony, lignum vitae, boxwood, partridge wood, cocus, etc. They are mostly sold by weight, and are obtainable in relatively small sizes only. Their close, dense grain makes them suitable for miniature work, but they are hard on the tools, long thin bevels being useless and liable to crumble. In fact engravers' burins are frequently used, at any rate on end grain.

Index